The Politically Incorrect Guide® to Immigration

Be sure to check out

The Politically Incorrect Guides® to...

The Politically Incorrect Guide® to
Immigration

John Zmirak and Al Perrotta

REGNERY
PUBLISHING
A Division of Salem Media Group

Portions of this book appeared previously at The Stream and at Modern Age, and are reprinted by permission.

Regnery® is a registered trademark of Salem Communications Holding Corporation

Cataloging-in-Publication data on file with the Library of Congress

ISBN 978-1-62157-673-0
e-book ISBN 978-1-62157-758-4

Published in the United States by
Regnery Publishing
A Division of Salem Media Group
300 New Jersey Ave NW
Washington, DC 20001
www.Regnery.com

Manufactured in the United States of America

10 9 8 7 6 5 4 3 2 1

Books are available in quantity for promotional or premium use. For information on discounts and terms, please visit our website: www.Regnery.com.

For Patty Fain, a most tolerant and forgiving older sister, and for Anthony Ottaviano, who introduced the young Niles Crane to garage bands
—John Zmirak

To my father, Albert B. Perrotta Sr., who so deeply instilled in me the idea that our gifts are to be used in service. He lived with music in his head, laughter on his lips, love in his heart and grace in his step. I aspire to live the same and I am beyond blessed to bear his name. And to my wife, Rusty Burns. Yes, you soak me with love and support. But I dedicate this book specifically to you because of your inspiration. You are, without a doubt, the most talented person I've ever met. But what separates you is the effort. The heart. The integrity. The push for excellence. It is how you turn amateurs into powerhouses, a decrepit bathroom into a glorious Shangri-la…and a carefree scribbler into an author, playwright, and managing editor. Yes, God gave me talent. But more crucially, He gave me you. And that has made all the difference in the world. This book is dedicated to you, with all my love.
—Al Perrotta

Contents

Why Americans Care so Much about This Issue

Immigration is perhaps the most divisive issue in America. What's telling about it is how it divides, and whom it splits from whom. For one thing, it divides those who know how to use "whom" correctly (and who insist upon it pedantically) from the rest of the population, who don't or won't. It divides the elites in both political parties from large parts of their traditional base. The Democrats' lurch toward open borders and xenomania is carving off large chunks of their base and handing it to Republicans, while Republican elites who listen to donors instead of voters on this issue are being sloughed off by the party like a rented tuxedo jacket after a bad wedding. Or do you expect John Kasich and Lindsey Graham to get a lot of votes in the next GOP presidential primaries?

Immigration is a complex policy issue with huge implications for our nation's future. It is also a deeply sensitive topic that taps into conflicting images and concepts of what America really is. It summons our memories of ancestors who came here with nothing. It evokes black-and-white mental pictures of forebears who came to our shores seeking the golden chance to be Americans, to better themselves and their families by a lifetime of hard work. Those contrast with TV clips of immigrants today who seem to arrive here expecting everything—at the taxpayer's expense, while waving the colorful flags of foreign nations.

One very public incident—it happened during a White House press conference—in 2017 nicely captured the shape of the controversy over immigration: the televised scuffle between CNN's Jim Acosta, who plays a reporter on TV, and White House speechwriter and big brain Stephen Miller. The topic? Immigration and the Statue of Liberty. Miller gave a reasoned presentation of Trump's immigration plan, which while imperfect, would vastly improve our legal regime for admitting newcomers. It serves the national interest, avoids invidious discrimination, and ends an absurd system created by Teddy Kennedy in 1965, apparently on a bar napkin after his sixth shot of Jameson.

In response, Acosta read a poem, "The New Colossus," by Emma Lazarus. It's a wonderful poem, actually. But it's just a poem. You know, like "'Twas the Night before Christmas." The words "Give me your tired, your poor," and so forth have exactly the same legal weight as

Now, Dasher! Now, Dancer! Now, Prancer and Vixen!
On, Comet! On, Cupid! On, Donner and Blitzen!

Miller responded by schooling Acosta on the poem itself. An educational smackdown so bad it's a surprise James Madison University didn't call up Acosta demanding its diploma back.

And the liberal media erupted. It is true, some admitted, that the poem by Emma Lazarus was not part of the original Statue of Liberty. (It's on a plaque that was put up later.) And that its embrace of mass immigration had nothing whatsoever to do with the meaning of the statue itself. *But it was wrong for Miller to know that.* That fact is a "favorite talking point" of the "Alt-Right"—whatever that means in this context, since nothing has ever shown that Miller is a racist.

So while the late addition of the Emma Lazarus poem to the Statue of Liberty is a fact, it's a *bad* fact. The kind you're not supposed to know. It's up there with the suicide rates of post-op transgenders, the body-parts trafficking of Planned Parenthood, the promiscuity of male homosexuals, and other examples of Crimethink.

Instead of that bad fact, the media would like to offer you some elevated emotions: the aw-shucks feeling that makes your throat catch when you read that lovely poem by Emma Lazarus. The wistful sense of gratitude that washes over you when you think of your immigrant ancestors. You flip through those sepia photos of them and wonder what it was like to go through life in a world of black and white.

We kid, but not entirely. The world we inhabit is so radically different from that of our great-grandparents, it's hard to imagine that they actually lived in color. Our country has changed in crucial ways.

When John Zmirak's maternal Irish ancestors left Cork, they were fleeing a hell on earth: a moonscape of dead potato plants littered with corpses, some of their mouths green from gnawing on grass for nourishment. They came in "coffin ships" to a New York City with no public welfare system, and only volunteer firefighters, who were corrupt, violent—and Irish.

People came half-starved, illiterate, many of them addicted to alcohol or accustomed to prostitution. The government didn't help them. It couldn't. They sank or swam, thrived or died. Only the Catholic Church offered material help—at the price of moral uplift. If a young girl stayed chaste, nuns would find her a job as a maid. If a young man stayed sober, some priest would call his cousin and find him a job as a policeman. Those who strayed were on their own. Many thousands sailed back home.

Darwinian conditions continued among some families, particularly where "drink" was an issue. Zmirak's grandmother gave birth eleven times (at home). Only five of her children lived past the age of three. His grandfather was an alcoholic and, alas, a taxi driver. Not the best work-life balance. But those were tougher times.

Zmirak's paternal grandfather fled the war-torn Habsburg Empire in 1916. He hopped on a U.S. Merchant Marine ship during World War I and offered to serve on vessels being hunted by German U-boats. He came to Manhattan and worked the rest of his life shoveling coal into an engine on a tugboat. He could never hope to be captain, because his English was never that good. Today his job would be illegal—it's too unhealthy.

Zmirak's father served in World War II but scorned the G.I. Bill, seeking out at his father's suggestion one of the only jobs that had never dried up in the Great Depression: postman. So John Zmirak Sr. carried mail on his back for thirty-seven years. (There were no carts back then.) And his son got to go to Yale. When Mr. Zmirak went on to work as a doorman in a fancy Park Avenue building, some of John's classmates actually lived there. "My dad hauls your luggage," he liked to point out to those guilt-harried liberals. John just thought it was cool.

That's America, folks. Our grandparents lived sepia-tinted lives. But we get to live in color. And living in color changes a lot things. Now we have workplace safety laws and minimum wages, unions and disparate-impact class-action discrimination lawsuits. And lavish welfare programs that enfold vast percentages of the population. We outsource much of our grunt work to other countries, where the citizens still live in black-and-white.

So we just don't need to import a million or so mostly unskilled workers every year. We don't know what to do with them. There already aren't enough attractive entry-level jobs to lure our own urban poor away from crime or welfare. What's more, we no longer know how to assimilate people—since we're now ashamed of our culture. We can't give honest answers to problems like Sharia. (The only honest answer, actually, is directions to the nearest international airport.)

And so we can't live out the lovely words that Emma Lazarus wrote. They don't apply here anymore. We're a grown-up, full-color country.

But much of the rest of the world still lives in the dreary shades of poverty and want. They lack the rule of law, or property rights, or a decent system of government, or the culture of entrepreneurship. They produce, every year, millions of unskilled and restless citizens who would like to come to America.

But grown-up, developed, full-color countries don't need them. America used to need low-skill immigrants, but now it doesn't. That's sad but true. If we take too many of them, we will share their homelands' fate: bankruptcy and chaos. (Especially since so many low-skill immigrants vote for Democrats, whose platform boils down to just that dystopian future—see California.)

What we can offer the poor of the world is our good will, our trade, our prayers, and our example. We can be a light unto the nations. And that's exactly what the vast green statue in New York Harbor, with her torch shining out as a beacon (not a beckon) to the rest of the world, was supposed to mean in the first place.

The Moral Problem

Each of us co-authors writes as a serious Christian, one (Zmirak) Catholic, the other (Perrotta) Evangelical. So we bring certain moral concerns to our discussion of this issue. Unfortunately, it is rare to find calm, thoughtful Christian commentary on immigration these days. The problem starts at the top. Too many religious leaders replace moral reasoning with *moralism*. That's the stance where you solve all the problems entailed in a complex question by *choosing the answer in advance*. You present your predetermined answer as an unconditional demand—say that it comes from God. Then it's easy to tar people who

★ ★ ★

Pulling Out All the Stops

Let's say your immigration plan has catastrophic consequences. Like Angela Merkel's open door to Muslim colonists. Then you can bring out the big guns. Start accusing anyone who objects of being a "consequentialist." If your opponents point to economic costs, blame them for putting "profits over people." If they cite any statistics, damn them for "reducing human beings to numbers."

object to your plan as immoral, disobedient disciples, haters. When people point out the moral complexities and practical problems that you've ignored, you've got an answer: they're callously "splitting hairs" *when the lives of poor refugees are at stake,* or coldly "utilitarian," *daring to think through* the likely results of the policy you're insisting on. Never mind that considering the justice of likely consequences is key to the moral virtue of prudence.

We could multiply examples of this kind of rhetoric. Start with Pope Francis's claim that opposition to Muslim mass migration into Europe puts immigration hawks in the same moral footing as Cain and King Herod (see chapter four). Or how about Bishop Daniel Flores of Brownsville, Texas, who compared deporting immigrants to aborting unborn children?[1] Does Flores realize that he equated the nation of Mexico with a medical waste dumpster? There are plenty of Protestant examples as well, alas. Russell Moore of the Southern Baptist Convention likes to make the absurd claim that "our Lord Jesus himself was a so-called "illegal immigrant."[2] Really? Exactly how? When his parents (to escape the real Herod) moved temporarily from the Roman province of Judaea to the Roman province of Egypt—then returned a few months later? Such sloppy, emotive rhetoric is everywhere in Christian circles. It suffocates rational thought and shames people into submission. You get the idea.

Tempers can get hot on the other side of the question, too. We hear people talk about "treason" and "selling out our country" in return for cheap labor, cheap votes, warm bodies in pews, or funding from George Soros.

There's a time and a place for heat, but maybe we need more light. We were recently pleased to glimpse some in, of all places, the liberal Jesuit magazine *America*. Pascal-Emmanuel Gobry published a piece there that's admirably balanced.[3] Sane and calm. It breathes the same spirit as the passages in the Catholic Catechism on immigration. Since too few Catholics consult that, let us quote it here:

> The more prosperous nations are obliged, to the extent they are able, to welcome the foreigner in search of the security and the means of livelihood which he cannot find in his country of origin. Public authorities should see to it that the natural right is respected that places a guest under the protection of those who receive him.
>
> Political authorities, for the sake of the common good for which they are responsible, may make the exercise of the right to immigrate subject to various juridical conditions, especially with regard to the immigrants' duties toward their country of adoption. Immigrants are obliged to respect with gratitude the material and spiritual heritage of the country that receives them, to obey its laws and to assist in carrying civic burdens.[4]

Gobry writes in the same spirit. He acknowledges, for instance, that the immigration debate is not just about benefits for and moral claims of immigrants. There are other stakeholders too—namely, citizens. As Gobry says:

> I do not know what I believe because there are genuine questions of both prudence and principle that remain unresolved. How many immigrants can any given society safely absorb? What are the empirical costs and benefits of immigration? (I have looked at a lot

of social science, and the answer is murky.) Are Christians not supposed to believe in the legitimacy of civil authority and non-totalitarian states, which cannot exist without borders? Are we not supposed to be skeptical of the desires of the rich and of big business, who in the West overwhelmingly support and benefit from expanded immigration? I am not sure how to settle these matters.

Gobry also raises crucial questions that most readers of *America* had probably never seen posed:

> I grant the Gospel imperative to "welcome the stranger." But here is the thing: The church's doctrine also supports the right of sovereign countries to have borders. It is one of the most basic duties of states to enforce their borders.... At some point, according to church doctrine, it is a country's right and even duty to say "No" to some perfectly nice people.
>
> My question is: What is that point? I mean that seriously. I would be much more comfortable with emotion-laden appeals to "welcome the stranger" if they were accompanied with some logic or rationale for the point at which welcoming the stranger becomes imprudent. Or do you favor completely open borders? And if you do, why not simply make the case for that?

We can't answer that question on behalf of pro-immigration activists. But we'd love to hear their answer.

Gobry poses an equally worthy question to people like us, who want to tighten our borders:

> What is distinctly Christian about your approach?... [T]he doctrine is not silent. It does call on us to make a specific moral

effort. Even if you are right empirically about the negative effects of increased immigration, it is still the case that the Gospel calls on us to show special, supererogatory concern for migrants and refugees. Put differently: What is it that would distinguish your ideal immigration regime from the ideal immigration regime of a completely secular person who happened to share your empirical analysis of the costs and benefits of immigration?[5]

It's an earnest inquiry, and worth an answer. Here's ours:

Nothing.

The immigration policy—and any other public policy—that we support as Christians is based on the wise, prudent application of *natural law.* That's the moral code that God wrote on everyone's heart. You don't need supernatural faith to know it, though grace certainly helps you to obey it. Natural law, not the gospel, is the proper basis for legislation in a pluralist society.

How fair is it to ask Jewish citizens (for instance) to bear the costs of a policy that's driven not by reason and justice, but by a specifically Christian notion of "generosity"? Not fair at all, we'd say. On a long list of issues, from abortion to euthanasia, from aid to the poor to just war theory and even same-sex marriage, natural law provides clear, consistent guidance. We should base our policy arguments in natural law, not sectarian doctrine.

Our Christian faith drives us, of course. It makes us see the importance of natural law, human dignity, and universal human rights. But all those things are knowable to non-believers, too. And that is why they should be the guides for our *public* policy. Would we really want specifically Christian doctrines dictating laws? If so, which Christian Church would interpret them? The Churches differ on many, many issues. Politicizing the gospel is a sure way to set them at each other's throat. That's why our Founders wisely forbade a national Church.

The place of Christians, specifically, in aiding immigrants isn't rewriting policy to suit the pope or the Presbyterians. It's to use our churches as places of welcome for those who come into the country legally. Evangelize them. Teach them English. Help them gain job skills. Find them babysitters for their kids. Help them assimilate. And do it with church-raised money, not federal funds obtained by becoming government contractors. That's what the churches should be doing—not grabbing for power to enforce the gospel via the government.

According to the Gallup Poll,[6] some seven hundred million people around the world want to leave their native countries. That is "more than the entire adult population of North and South America combined." But relax, relax. *Only 165 million* of those want to come to America, Gallup reassures us. They would make up half our population. Since most are poor, they'd bankrupt every social program we have in a matter of months.

Here are some stark, honest questions you should ask of anyone who claims that illegal immigrants have a moral right to stay in America—or that we may not reduce legal immigration totals, rebalancing them in favor of skilled immigrants and against those from countries where terrorism is common and Sharia widely accepted:

- Do we have the right to say "No" to any of those 165 million people?
- If so, based on what? Our national interest, maybe?
- Are we allowed to seek the best interests of America, even if it inconveniences foreign citizens whose presence here breaks our laws?
- Regarding so-called "Dreamers," who were brought to the United States illegally as children, if parents steal something of value and give it to their kids, do they get to keep it, because they're innocent?

- If that applies to the trust funds Bernie Madoff set up for his grandchildren, why not to U.S. citizenship?
- We can only accept a finite number of immigrants. So how many Middle Eastern Christian refugees and Korean physicists who followed the legal immigration rules do you want to turn away? You know, to make room for these kids whose parents broke the law?

Does Christianity really teach that nations may not protect their own citizens first? The citizens whom their country taxes? Drafts into wars? Regulates, relies on, and—when they violate its laws—imprisons? By the very same logic, we shouldn't take care of our own children before we look out for total strangers. If that's true, then it's wrong to set aside college funds, vacation money, or cash for piano lessons for our own flesh and blood—as long as anyone, anywhere, is hungry somewhere on Earth.

On this same logic, nations that have followed smart economic policies and inherited healthy political cultures may not protect what they have while wishing others well and offering help as it seems prudent. Nope. We must open up our homes to every mental patient, no matter the damage they do. However much terrorism the influx of Muslims brings into Europe, that's the cross we must bear. And we must impose it on our non-Christian neighbors. Because the pope or some Soros-funded pastor says so.

★ ★ ★

Misreading the Gospel

The idea that Christians must embrace mass immigration is the kind of misreading of the gospel that the Gnostics used to produce in the early Church. You know, the people who demanded that every Christian be dirt-poor and celibate, or else they were betraying the gospel. It's bad enough to impose such heretical readings of Scripture on Christians. To use the force of the state to require that every citizen obey misguided theology is even worse.

A Divided Country

Restoring order to our chaotic immigration system would do a lot of important things. It would save taxpayers billions. It would give more opportunity to the native-born working class. It would restore respect for the law and for American citizenship. But here is the most crucial good it would accomplish: it would help to *stabilize* our country. We need that more than we have in decades—in part because of out-of-control illegal immigration, but in larger part because of native-grown forces that are sowing division among us.

On so many issues, the Left seems determined to drive the rest of the country into rebellion against their ever-more-ridiculous demands. They have dialed up to eleven their outrage against anything that smacks of old-fashioned American values. They are persecuting Christian bakers. Tech employees who disagree with their boss's politics. Conservative and even moderate college profs. Protesters at the College of William and Mary shouted down a speaker from the ACLU. *Because the ACLU defends the First Amendment Freedom of Speech.* The social justice warriors are on a quest to find ever new outrages to launch against existing mores. To find the last few surviving strands of Christian faith—or just of rational thinking—and rip them out by the roots. We're haters if we put up any resistance to the craziness hijacking our educational institutions, our legal system, and our country. Or if we raise any objections to welcoming another million-plus foreigners, legal and illegal, into the country *every year* to take sides in our ongoing culture war.

Before we could wrap our heads around same-sex marriage, BAM! We were anti-trans bigots for wanting single-sex bathrooms. Then BAM! Why are we so hateful that we don't want to fund sex change operations for soldiers? How cruel and harsh can we be, to favor policies that liberals also favored, say, *two years ago*?

We need a break. That's the main reason people voted for Donald Trump. He was gruff. Politically incorrect. Even kind of a cad. Maybe he would have a thick enough skin. He'd be rude enough to endure all the abuse. To say "Heck, no!" to the next set of crackpot demands.

One of the easiest ways to destabilize a country: flood it with newcomers. Want to wreck the place quickly and irreversibly? Make them openly hostile colonists. Like the hundreds of thousands of strutting Sharia Muslims. You know, the guys who are now harassing, shaming, and raping women all over Europe.

Fortunately, America doesn't sit close to any massive Muslim population centers. But newcomers need not be hostile to have an impact. Just large, large numbers of people all coming at once will do the trick. Especially if your country has lost the techniques for assimilating them. Or if it has become too self-hating even to try.

CHAPTER ONE

Houston, We've Got a Problem

In the month we finished writing this book, two events appeared on TV that, juxtaposed, illustrate why Americans are worried. And angry. And willing to make surprising political choices, like electing Donald Trump.

A minivan terrorizes Americans, singling out non-white children, threatening to run them down and kill them. As the young people flee for safety, we see right-wing slogans on the back of the vehicle, and its driver pulls off unpunished.

A truck barrels down a bike path in Manhattan, targeting pedestrians of every race. It continues for seven blocks and kills eight people as its driver shouts "Allahu Akbar!" out the window, before he is shot by a cop.

What's the difference between these two events?

One was fictional—hatched in the fevered brain of left-wingers working to get a Democrat elected governor in Virginia. And the other really happened.

The first was a Latino Victory campaign ad trying to tar squishy moderate Republican candidate Ed Gillespie with the guilt of a white supremacist who had charged Antifa demonstrators in Charlottesville, Virginia, in the summer of 2017.[1] (Maybe it worked; Gillespie lost.)

Did you know?

★ Immigrant-headed households take 57 percent more food assistance than other households

★ Average cost in welfare to every illegal immigrant–headed household: $5,692

★ "The Wall" would cost $12–15 billion—and save almost $64 billion over the first ten years

★ Competition from immigrants costs American workers $450 billion a year

The second was a real terrorist attack, by a winner of America's "Diversity Visa" lottery, a Muslim supremacist who followed up the murderous attack by pledging allegiance to ISIS from the safety of his New York City hospital bed. The attack was followed, as usual, by official denials that Islamist terrorism has any connection to Islam, and warnings against "Islamophobia."[2]

The first, the fantasy, is how the Left sees America. The second is an instance of what has really begun happening here.

Immigration is one of the most controversial topics in American politics. And no wonder, because the elites who have made "multiculturalism" and "diversity" into our nation's post-Christian civic religion keep beating it into our heads with threats, shame campaigns, and manipulative messaging.

Will it work? The election of Donald Trump suggests it might not. Like an Indian tribe whose past chiefs were selling its land to the English piece by piece in return for bottles of whiskey, we might just have woken up.

Our elites want us to believe that mass, low-skill immigration is a force of nature, like sunspots or evolution, over which we have no influence. In fact, as this book will show, our current immigration regime is the fruit of political choices—some of them reckless and short-sighted, some deliberate and destructive.

We still can make choices about where immigration takes us in the future. There is nothing inevitable about it. We, the People, have the power.

Immigration: Force of Nature or a Political Choice?

Step back for a moment from the saccharine prefab stories about foreign-born "Dreamers." Bracket the moralizing of opinion manufacturers whose lifestyles aren't affected, or who judge public policy by its impact on cheap exotic restaurants and low-priced nannies. Let's look at what immigration is really about.

It's about people. And culture. It's about the kind of country our ancestors helped to build, and what kind of country we will leave to our descendants. Aren't those legitimate issues for debate in a democracy? Indeed, they lie at the very heart of politics. Man is a political animal—by which Aristotle meant that we normally live in community. The most basic unit is the family: man-woman-children. (However much that primordial truth is under savage, sustained attack today.)

But families have to educate their children, which usually means a school. They don't live on isolated rural estates guarded by moats. That means a neighborhood. They get services from the government and contribute to it in taxes. That means politics. Any political change that radically affects the schools your kids attend, the neighborhood you live in, and the effects that government has on your life is fair game for debate.

As this book will show, immigration has massive impacts on all those things, so even from the perspective of just making your way through life while minding your own business, you're obliged to face the effects of mass, low-skill immigration. But look beyond tending your garden. Most of us take some pride in our country and want it to thrive. We treasure its founding principles and pray for its success. We want to see ordered liberty survive for future generations—for our own children's sake, but also because it adds meaning to all our lives. We identify with our country, honor its flag, tear up at its national anthem, and enlist to fight in its wars. Think of it this way: If someone told you that America was going split up into ten or twenty mutually suspicious mini-states—or be defeated in a war, occupied by a foreign power, and forced to renounce our Constitution and our commitment to the principles in the Declaration of Independence—wouldn't it break your heart? Even if you were promised that it wouldn't happen until after you and everyone you knew was dead?

We bet it would. You would feel that something great had perished—something in which you had played a part, that had shaped your life and blessed you, that your ancestors had honored and you hope your kids will inherit. If you had a 240-year-old tree in your yard, wouldn't you feel some compunction about cutting it down for use in a paper mill? Or letting it die of an easily preventable disease? We feel the same way about our country. In fact, we feel much more deeply, because a country is the product of the greatest thing on God's Earth—human souls, working together, striving to live in common in ordered liberty, the only condition worthy of God-given human dignity. That is the shining vision our Founders left us.

To carry this vision on, we need to be good citizens. Any argument about immigration must hinge on what that means. What is a good citizen of this specific place, the United States of America? What virtuous habits does our country rely on us to practice, in order for our rare and fragile system of government to flourish? Which assumptions, practices, and beliefs make it possible to have a mostly free country with decentralized power and strong property rights? How can we preserve the rights to life, liberty, and the pursuit of happiness? What bad habits—if we took them up or massively imported them—would make all that impossible? Would force us to adopt a much more bureaucratic and even authoritarian form of government, like most governments in the world, just to keep basic order in the streets? What makes the United States different from Syria? From Mexico? From Venezuela?

Surely these are among the central questions that citizens of a democracy must think about. Yet the taboo on talking about immigration requires that we pretend such issues don't matter. We are expected to act as if human beings were not just equal in the eyes of God (true), but interchangeable, like auto parts (false). We are told that every religious belief, political habit, ideology, or cultural practice is functionally equivalent. Above all, we must not judge them, must not express a preference for (say) tolerant-minded, hard-working Christians over angry, militant, Sharia-minded Muslims. We can't limit the number of Latin Americans we admit—good people, no doubt, but their whole life experience has been shaped by corrupt governments in bed with narco-terrorists.

Multiculturalism demands that we bend over backwards to ignore all that we might find unsettling about another culture and consistently scourge ourselves, our nation, and our ancestors for our flaws. This ideology pretends that the American creed of equal rights for all demands that we extend the privilege of citizenship promiscuously to all—never considering the impact that immigrants, in large enough numbers, may have on our nation and its liberties. On our own rights. On our tax rates and our neighborhoods, our elections and our kids' schools. We're forbidden by this strange diktat to consider the most important questions of politics.

Maybe we don't listen to the multiculturalists, but instead to the economists. To those who won't look beyond the narrow terms of their economic specialty, the only questions immigration poses are of aggregate supply and demand. More immigrants mean more consumers and producers, which is a good thing because they boost our aggregate numbers. Every new arrival in America is an interchangeable production-and-consumption unit who will pay into our Social Security system and boost our national growth. How can you have too much of a good thing? By this logic, the *Economist* magazine has argued for decades that Europe must solve the problem of its aging population not by boosting birth rates, which might interfere with sexual freedom, but by opening its doors to massive influx from the Middle East. Cue the unintended consequences—including the 2015–2016 New Year's Eve mass sexual assaults in Cologne and other European cities, which the *Economist* didn't seem to see coming. But they didn't affect its position: the magazine was still doubling down in July 2017.[3]

The economism of the *Economist* degrades people by treating their culture, morals, creeds, and customs as utterly unimportant. Yet those things constitute the vast bulk of our existence. Our willingness to work and eagerness to consume are only a small part of what makes us human. We are more than strong backs and hungry mouths. Yet that is how narrow, economic-minded types insist on seeing us.

Those of us who worry about the impact of immigration are much more holistic. We consider the entire person—his habits, virtues, and deepest beliefs—as of the utmost importance. We honestly face the impact that un- or anti-American cultural practices, when multiplied in the millions, can have on our fragile country. We respect foreign people enough to take them seriously as people just like us. And sometimes that means we have to tell them, "No." We won't act like the Left and give every comer a pat on the head and a raft of government programs. We won't act like the pro-business, open-borders Right and reduce human beings to interchangeable integers. It's not just false. It's immoral.

Now that we've established that immigration is a perfectly mainstream subject for concern, what about it exactly concerns people? Of course, different citizens have different priorities. Some people are more alarmed by one aspect of this issue than others. That's fine. In this regard, the immigration control movement can say in all sincerity, "Our diversity is our strength." In the rest of this chapter, we'll unfold, one by one, the key aspects of immigration policy that concern Americans willing to face the deplorable truth about our current immigration regime. We will review the legitimate reasons that motivate most people who consider immigration a crucial issue, and also the darker motives that move a few extremists, whose intolerance is used by open-borders moralists to smear everyone else who cares about the issue.

National Sovereignty

As Reagan famously said, "A nation that cannot control its borders is not a nation." Believe it or not, that matter-of-fact statement has become controversial. At some American colleges, it might be treated as hate speech. So let's examine why it is true—and the motives of those who pretend that it's false.

What is government? It is the organization of people to defend the common good, protect individual rights, and promote the legitimate self-interest of a nation's inhabitants as a group. Government is the means of guaranteeing a monopoly of the use of violent force (except in immediate self-defense), and restricting that violence within the scope of the rule of law.

If a state cannot control who enters its borders, it has no way to guarantee that everyone present in the country is willing to obey those laws, pay taxes, or fulfill their other civic responsibilities. Indeed, it might not even have any record of who is present in the country at all—making it impossible to enforce any such duties or track down criminals. And in fact, today there are somewhere around ten million people present in the United States illegally, for whom all that is true. They don't have legitimate driver's licenses, auto insurance, health insurance, Social Security records, or any of the myriad of other legal records that the government uses to enforce the law and hold people liable when they injure others.

To choose just a basic dollars-and-cents issue: If your new car is hit by an illegal immigrant driving without insurance, who pays to replace it? You do, or your insurance company. Likewise, your own insurance, not his, will have to pay for your medical expenses—which might go on for the rest of your life, depending on how serious the accident is. The more uninsured drivers there are on the road, the higher your rates will have to be to accommodate this reality. How do you sue someone who is here illegally and has no assets in his name? Just list all the reasons why we have tort law and traffic laws in the first place, and you immediately see the problem of having ten million people effectively exempted from those laws.[4]

Illegal immigrants themselves are not protected by our labor, health, and safety laws. They work for cash that is not taxed or reported to the government, in conditions set at their employers' whims. They do not have the option (for fear of being deported) of reporting dangerous or unhealthy conditions. They have no insurance for workplace injuries. In effect, they are working under the same legal conditions as laborers did in 1880, before government regulations were imposed to protect workers from deadly or dangerous conditions and exploitative rates of pay. Wherever employers can get away with using illegal immigrants, such laws (including the minimum wage) effectively do not exist.

A radical libertarian might consider that a good thing, but most of us believe that such laws were passed for good reasons. If you wish to repeal them, make your case to the public. But there's no justification for carving out lawless zones where these valid laws are simply evaded. And of course the presence of a large illegal workforce that will work under nineteenth-century conditions has an impact on the wages of other Americans—more on the economic impact of immigration later. For now, just think about what it means for the legitimacy of policies democratically enacted by legislatures—and the sanctity of the rule of law—that millions of American employers simply flout them with impunity.

Apart from anarchists or the most extreme libertarians, few would claim that a nation has no right to patrol its borders and control who comes and goes. Making such a claim and applying it equally to the United States and to Mexico, to Germany and to Tunisia, would require too much intellectual consistency. It would also be impossible to defend. Instead, pro-immigration activists follow the multiculturalist strategy of denying only rich, Western, or majority-white countries the right to enforce border laws. They cite past discrimination, colonialism, "white privilege," or long-settled land disputes (such as those that were ended by the 1846–1848 Mexican-American War) to condemn only a select set of countries for practicing this routine basic function of a government. Hence the same activist who will label the removal of illegal immigrants from the United States "ethnic cleansing" will say nothing when Mexico or Santo Domingo deports people, as they do energetically.

National Security

While we face nowhere near the level of terrorist attacks endured by nations like France and Germany, which recklessly admitted millions of Muslim immigrants, a significant number of terrorist strikes in the United States are being committed by immigrants or "refugees." The Heritage Foundation's online publication, The Daily Signal has a helpful—if sobering—tracker of all such terror attacks (and foiled terror attempts) from 2001 up through October 2016. Here are excerpts—covering just the last two years—selected from that archive:

December 2, 2015

U.S. citizen Syed Rizwan Farook and his wife Tashfeen Malik, originally from Pakistan, attacked the Inland Regional Center for disabilities development, killing 14 of Farook's coworkers. (The same co-workers who had thrown Malik a baby shower.)....

Reports show Malik had devoted allegiance to ISIS. FBI has since noted that the couple had been radicalized for "quite some time."

Neighbors who had seen suspicious activity did not contact police. They didn't want to be labeled "islamophobic."

January 6, 2016

Omar Faraj Saeed Al Hardan, a Palestinian born in Iraq who entered the U.S. as a refugee in 2009, was initially charged with

★ ★ ★
Overstaying Their Welcome

Have you heard of 9/11 Families for a Safe & Strong America? It's a group formed by survivors of those killed in the worst terrorist attack in U.S. history. Too many forget that all of the eleven hijackers on September 11, 2001, were immigrants. In fact, they had all entered the United States legally on tourist or student visas—and three of them had simply overstayed.[5] There was no system for tracking and removing them then, and a decade and a half later, there still isn't one now. What is the point of having a visa system at all, if once people enter the United States they can stay as long as they like?

attempting to provide support to ISIS and lying to officials on his citizenship application and associated interview. According to Special Agent Herman Wittliff, Al Hardan wanted to set off bombs using cellphone detonators at two malls in Houston, Texas, and told an FBI informant that he wanted to imitate the Boston Marathon bombing.

June 12, 2016

[Son of Afghan immigrants] Omar Mateen attacked the Pulse nightclub in Orlando with multiple firearms, killing 49 and injuring more than 50 before police stormed the building and killed Mateen. According to the FBI, Mateen talked to a 911 operator three times to announce his allegiance to ISIS during the attack, as well as his solidarity with other Islamist terrorists, including the Boston Marathon bombers.

September 17, 2016

On September 17, Dahir Ahmed Adan [a native of Kenya who had been admitted to the United States at the age of two as a refugee and later became an American citizen] entered a mall in St. Cloud, Minnesota, dressed as a security guard, and began stabbing individuals before an off-duty police officer shot and killed him. According to police, Adnan asked at least one person if they were a Muslim before attacking them and made statements regarding Allah during the attack.

September 17, 2016

The morning of September 17, a pipe bomb exploded in Seaside Park, New Jersey. At around 8:30 P.M. on the same day, a high explosive pressure-cooker bomb exploded in Manhattan, leaving at least 31 individuals injured. Other bombs were located in Manhattan and at a train station in New Jersey.

The investigation led to [Afghanistan-born, naturalized U.S. citizen] Ahmad Rahami being subdued after shooting and injuring two police officers before being shot himself.

November 28, 2016

Abdul Razak Ali Artan drove a car into a crowd of pedestrians at Ohio State University and then attacked them with a knife, injuring 11.[6]

OSU jihad attacker Abdul Razak Ali Artan was a radicalized Muslim refugee from Somalia who was intent on avenging the "wrongs" that America (and other countries) supposedly commit against Muslims. The United States grants refugee status, in accord with international law, to people fleeing persecution and violence in their home countries. By that same international law, those people should go to the "first safe country" where they can escape the chaos.

How many Sunni Muslim countries are closer to Somalia than the United States? A short list would include Saudi Arabia, Qatar, Egypt, Dubai, Bahrain, Tunisia, Algeria, Morocco, Bosnia, and Jordan. Yet these nations accept few refugees. Puritanical Saudi Arabia or early ISIS-sponsor Qatar would clearly be a better home for the likes of Artan.

But the broken U.S. refugee vetting system, and a lavishly funded domestic industry that

★ ★ ★

The Exception That Proves the Rule

Rapidly radicalizing Turkey is one Sunni country that does accept refugees—and then it passes them on to Europe, wielding the flow of migrants as a weapon. Turkey threatens to dump a fresh influx of military-age male colonists on Germany and Italy if the EU doesn't grant Turkey's latest demands, including freedom of travel for the whole population of Turkey throughout every nation in the EU.[7]

★ ★ ★

Who's Paying?

Why did Catholic Charities of Dallas under then–Bishop (now Cardinal) Kevin Farrell house Abdul Razak Ali Artan and his family?[8] The official story is that the Church is engaged in a Christian mission of mercy. Let's look at that claim more closely. As we explain in depth in chapter four, 97 cents of every dollar that the Church and Catholic agencies spend on resettling refugees comes from federal money.[9] Catholic Charities of Dallas, for instance, received $4,980,358 in federal money for immigration and refugee services in 2014. It spent $3,999,734 on refugees, and the rest on things like advocacy for illegal immigrants. And salaries, of course. Dallas Catholic Charities' gross receipts that year were $15,411,063. Almost exactly half of that money ($7,770,795) went to paying staff.[10]

In 2014, Bishop Farrell was the toast of the Catholic and mainstream media for housing in a Catholic retreat center the family members contaminated by an African migrant dying of Ebola who had lied his way into the United States and infected staff at a Dallas hospital. The Catholic News Agency gushed that Farrell had "offered them shelter in the name of Christ." The bishop made his name internationally with this resonant phrase: "[W]e don't help because someone is Catholic, we help because we are Catholic and that is what we are called to do."[11]

We saw social media comparisons between Bishop Farrell and St. Damien of Molokai, who cared for abandoned lepers until he died of the disease himself. In fact, no nursing nuns had any contact with the contaminated family members. Nor, it seems, did Bishop Farrell. We saw no press reports saying who was funding these patients' care. But given the fact that virtually all immigrant services provided by the Dallas Diocese rely on federal funds, it was likely a federally funded operation.

This is not exactly Christian charity. But it's excellent PR.

profits from it, instead put Artan in Ohio—where he could avenge the wrongs committed against Muslims anywhere in the world (he wrote on social media about the abuse of Muslims in Burma) on helpless American citizens.

Why were Abdul Razak Ali Artan, his mother, and six siblings transported at U.S. taxpayer expense first to Dallas, Texas, and then to Ohio? Clearly something in the system is broken—or someone in it deeply interested in forcibly "diversifying" America with thousands of politicized Muslims from terrorism-wracked countries. As Polizette points out, the number of Somali refugees admitted to America increased 250 percent under President Obama[12]—this despite the documented links between Somali refugees and the al Qaeda–affiliated terrorist group Al Shabaab, which threatened terrorist attacks on the Mall of America in 2015 in solidarity with ISIS.

Fake Refugees, Real Colonists and Conquerors

There is no reason for the United States or any Western country to accept a single Muslim refugee ever again. The very meaning of "refugee"—and the justification for accepting them outside of our normal immigration quotas and without regard to our national interests—depends on the fact that someone's life is directly in danger. But that danger vanishes the moment he sets foot in what international law recognizes as the "first safe country." There are no countries bordering the United States where Muslims are persecuted, so the proper number of Muslim refugees for the United States to take is zero. For almost 100 percent of so-called refugees who claim to be from Syria (for instance), that first safe country is Turkey—a vast and comparatively wealthy Sunni Muslim nation that could easily accept and assimilate all real refugees from Syria. Instead Turkey is dumping those economic migrants on the West, cannily predicting that they will increase Islamic influence in Europe.

Likewise, Algeria or Egypt could accept any real refugees from Libya. Any migrant who ignores the road to Cairo and instead sets forth on a boat for Greece or Italy is not a real refugee in search of asylum from chaos and persecution. He—like any Syrian "refugee" who passes through Turkey on his way to greener pastures in Germany or France—is an economic migrant, looking for either a job or a berth on European or American welfare programs, and there is no moral or legal reason to accept him. We say

★ ★ ★

Importing a Different World View

Jesus died for our sins; Muhammad conquered infidels for Allah. The contrast is that stark and basic.

"him" because a shockingly high percentage of these migrants are young men of military age—while the real Christian and Yazidi refugees from Iraq and Syria huddle in miserable transit camps replete with old people, women, and children.

What the world is seeing is not a refugee crisis but an Islamic colonization, led—like the Spanish conquest of Mexico—by young, able men who have come to scout out territory and claim it. These are not desperate civilians fleeing a war; they are the new conquistadors.

And we have seen their first massacres of the natives: in Paris every six weeks or so, at the Boston Marathon, at Fort Hood, and in a hundred other Western cities. We know that there will be more. ISIS has promised us more, boasting that it seeded the masses of "refugees" with its operatives to commit them.

But it's even worse than that. Forget the ISIS agents hiding among the refugees. Immigrant populations foster "homegrown" terrorists in the countries that have taken them in. Every Islamic population is a breeding ground for jihad, the holy war that stands at the heart of the Islamic faith as the cross does at the heart of Christianity. And we have invited Muslim populations to take up residence in our country.

When a young Muslim man feels dissatisfied with his lot in life, or humiliated by the need to adapt to Western ways, there is always a Saudi-funded mosque where he can go to find other young men who share his rage. They will have direct connections to terrorist organizations, and he will be guided to the vast literature of jihad that explains why killing infidels and subjugating their countries is the duty of every Muslim.[13]

President Obama ignored the clear message of the Paris massacres and doubled down on his anti-Christian policy, accepting tens of thousands of migrants who are Sunni Muslims, just like ISIS, while denying that the hunted Iraqi and Syrian Christians are the victims of genocide. Obama scoffed at the governors of states who demanded an end to the influx and lectured citizens that it's "un-American" to favor Christian refugees—who have no safe refuge anywhere in the Middle East—over Muslims who could safely resettle in more than a dozen Sunni Arab countries.

The same arguments moved courts to violate the Constitution and throw out President Trump's executive orders intended to correct Obama's policies. Even though the reason for the mass persecution of more than a million Christians is explicitly religious, these judges told us, we cannot take religion into account when welcoming refugees. That's odd, considering that the definition of refugee in international law is someone who "owing to well-founded fear of being persecuted for reasons of race, *religion*, nationality, membership of a particular social group or political opinion, is outside the country of his nationality..." [emphasis added].[14] If refugees are defined by religion, then why can't we take religion into account when deciding which refugees to admit? Would it have violated the First Amendment to favor Jewish émigrés from Hitler's Europe? (Alas, FDR's State Department refused to accept those persecuted Jews, letting thousands perish.)

In a situation where we ought to be favoring Christian refugees—who don't pose a special threat to our national security, and who have no safe countries to resort to in their own neighborhood—we're taking in even fewer of them than their proportion in the population of their home countries would dictate. Ten percent of Syrians are Christians but only about 2.5% of the refugees we have taken are Christian. Why is that? As Faith McDonnell explained at The Stream,

> When Christians flee as refugees they cannot go to UN-run refugee camps because there they face the same persecution and terror from which they fled. If they are not in the refugee camps

★ ★ ★

Screening for Religion—or Looks

The most popular and deeply false talking point among the supporters of mass Muslim migration to the United States? That restricting immigrants from Muslim nations somehow violates those migrants' First Amendment rights. But non-citizens don't have the rights of citizens. They have the same natural rights as we do, of course, but they no more have a First Amendment right to settle in United States so they can practice their religion here than they have a Second Amendment right to carry firearms in Texas, or a Nineteenth Amendment right to vote in our elections provided they're women. As we'll see in chapter two, an earlier generation of Americans worried that the Vatican would exert undue political influence on Catholic immigrants pushed successfully for the U.S. citizenship oath to include a clause by which the migrant pledges to "entirely renounce and abjure all allegiance and fidelity to any foreign prince, potentate, state, or sovereignty." That was meant to cover the papacy, as every Catholic immigrant knew. No court ever found that citizenship oath unconstitutional. In fact, the United States has a sovereign right to choose immigrants by any criteria whatsoever. No foreign person is entitled to live in the United States of America. We could, if we wished to, enact entirely aesthetic criteria—only accepting immigrants whom a panel of celebrity judges found to be just as attractive as Melania Trump. It would be stupid. But entirely constitutional.

they are not included in the application process for asylum. The U.S. State Department knows this, but continues to allow the office of the UN High Commissioner for Refugees (UNHCR) to select refugees for asylum with no regard to the endangered Christians and other religious minorities. According to statements in the *Sunday Express* from an ISIS defector and aid workers in the UN camps, ISIS is sending teams of trained assassins disguised as refugees to kidnap and kill Christians....

The blame is not just with the United Nations and the Obama administration. U.S. organizations who resettle refuges are also to blame. This includes Christian groups that resist any focus on

Christian victims of ISIS, and oppose actions by Congress to welcome not just economic migrants but also Christians and other religious minorities victimized by ISIS.[15]

Should Americans simply accept that every year there will be a dozen or so successful terrorist attacks by immigrants or their U.S.-born children? Is this the price we must pay for "diversity," defined as cheap labor, exotic ethnic restaurants, and a warm fuzzy feeling of self-congratulation? No major American politician has quite been bold enough to say so. But that's the unspoken message of leaders who loudly oppose reasonable measures— such as President Trump's executive orders—aimed at limiting immigration from terrorist-ridden nations.

In Europe, left-wing multiculturalists who control the main political parties lack the shame even to dissemble about these issues. They openly say that terrorism is the unhappy price which native citizens must pay for multiculturalism. As Breitbart London reported,

> Emmanuel Macron [elected French president in 2017] has described terrorism as an "imponderable problem" which will be "part of our daily lives for the years to come".
>
> Speaking in a French radio interview reported by The Guardian newspaper, the centre left En Marche! candidate appeared to echo former Prime Minister Manuel Valls's controversial statements following the Nice lorry attack on Bastille Day 2016, in which a Tunisian migrant mowed down 434 men, women, and children, killing 87.
>
> "Times have changed and we should learn to live with terrorism," Valls said at the time. The comments led to the socialist being cursed and jeered in public, and played a prominent role in terminating his own hopes of a presidential run.[16]

Just how dangerous is the current U.S. policy of accepting unvettable "refugees" from nations that breed terrorists? Progressives don't want you to find out. They don't even want the U.S. government to know the answer to that deplorable question. As Neil Munro reported at Breitbart, "Progressive lawyers and judges have frozen the Department of Homeland Security's effort to minimize security threats from each year's wave of government-approved refugees, even though the FBI says it is investigating and watching 300 foreign radicals who were invited into the country via the refugee programs."[17]

Nor are Muslim countries rife with terrorism the only security threat. Our largest source of immigrants is Mexico, a nation where narco-terrorist organizations have infiltrated, terrorized, or paralyzed much of the law enforcement infrastructure. Governors of states, police chiefs, crusading politicians, and rival gang members are routinely kidnapped, tortured, and murdered. According to CNN, in 2016 Mexico earned the tragic distinction of being the "second-deadliest country in the world":

> As Syria, Iraq and Afghanistan dominated the news agenda, Mexico's drug wars claimed 23,000 lives during 2016—second only to Syria, where 50,000 people died as a result of the civil war.
>
> "This is all the more surprising, considering that the conflict deaths [in Mexico] are nearly all attributable to small arms," said John Chipman, chief executive and director-general of the International Institute for Strategic Studies (IISS), which issued its annual survey of armed conflict on Tuesday.[18]

Defenders of our immigration status quo like to airbrush such statistics, and the threat posed by a de facto open border—which is effectively controlled at many points by people-smugglers connected to drug cartels. However, when Mexicans or Central Americans slip into the country and claim to be "refugees" from the chaos caused by these drug wars, the same progressives will pull these numbers out as proof that these civilians are victims of "persecution" who deserve permanent asylum in the United States.

Cultural Collapse, Political Hijack

Of course, few Americans will be directly affected by acts of terrorism, narco- or otherwise. Few will be personally murdered by jihadis or members of drug cartels. The indirect costs of mass immigration from chaotic countries are much vaster and harder to estimate. In just eight years of the George W. Bush presidency, the United States spent $1.8 trillion in the so-far unsuccessful "Global War on Terror."[19] This does not include the enormous costs and inconveniences imposed on U.S. air travel by the need for increased security, just to name one side effect. Terrorism can be countered, to some degree, by aggressive policing and domestic surveillance. But those measures impose costs on Americans' liberty and privacy—which should also be reckoned as part of the price for our lax immigration policies toward countries that export jihadi extremists and violent criminals.

Less tangible but much more serious impacts that mass immigration has on America are its dilution of our culture and the change it has caused in our electorate. Put bluntly, we inherited a country founded on a set of British values—including the "Anglo-American liberties" enjoyed in every nation of the Anglosphere. By importing large numbers of people every year from cultures that don't share those values and failing to assimilate them, we endanger the very roots of American freedom, order, and prosperity.

If a social engineer were consciously trying to end the American experiment, he could not come up with a more sure-fire method than this: import each year a million future voters and parents who believe in one or more of the following:

- Socialism and the massive redistribution of wealth
- The superiority of their religion to all others, and the duty of believers to wage jihad against the infidel
- Some anti-American nationalism or tribalism suffused with deep grudges against Anglo culture and the American government
- The assumption that government institutions will always be hopelessly corrupt
- Latino "familism"—the notion that it is a person's duty to look out only for members of his immediate family, not the broader community—or the Middle Eastern loyalty system expressed in the Bedouin proverb: "I and my brothers against my cousins, I and my cousins against the world"[20]
- The idea that wealth is always the fruit of inherited privilege and state-backed cronyism

British politician Daniel Hannan has carefully documented how the greatest political blessing that we residents of the "Anglosphere"—from Canada to India, from Australia to the Falkland Islands—enjoy is the fruit of the political principles, personal sacrifices, and prudent decisions of particular people. Our benefactors? The rebels and preachers, barons and burghers who resisted the arbitrary power of kings and fought for religious, political, and economic freedom. These distinct people, at distinct times and places, undertook political actions with enormous moral consequences, which generations of schoolchildren used to be dutifully drilled to remember: Runnymede, the Glorious Revolution, the abolition of the slave trade. All these political events grew out of certain stubborn beliefs, which we can boil down to one principle: that the dignity of each human being

A Book You're Not Supposed to Read

Adios America: The Left's Plan to Turn Our Country into a Third World Hellhole by Ann Coulter (Regnery, 2015).

affirmed by Christian theology has political implications, which philosophers such as John Locke presented in secular form as the inalienable rights to "life, liberty and property."

As we study less of this history with each generation, it is all too easy for us to take these privileges for granted, to assume that because (as our theology teaches us) every person deserves them, that it is only natural that they

A Book You're Not Supposed to Read

Inventing Freedom: How the English-Speaking Peoples Made the Modern World by Daniel Hannan (Broadside Books, 2013).

enjoy them. But if we read the chronicles of the centuries and survey not just non-Western civilizations but even most Western nations for most of their history, we will learn something quite different. In fact it is highly unusual for human life to be treated with unconditional respect, for citizens to be protected from arbitrary arrest and to be free to speak their minds, for the work of our hands and our brains to belong to us and our families, exempt from unfair confiscation. Life, liberty, and the right to enjoy the fruits of our labor are what God intends for us—as we Westerners grow up believing. But in cold fact, murder, bullying, and theft are too frequently the norm. How many newcomers accustomed to living that way can the United States absorb each year without being transformed for the worse?

U.S. elections are already being reshaped, and skewed to the Left, by the relentless influx of people whose families and cultural background incline them to favor big government, wealth redistribution, and centralized power over the classic Anglo-American preference for self-reliance, property rights, and localism. Before we get into the numbers, remember this: Democratic stronghold California was once the state that gave Ronald Reagan and Richard Nixon their start in politics. Now the state is so far Left that the election of Donald Trump led to widespread calls for secession from the Union—and much more seriously, to moves by dozens of city mayors to openly defy U.S. immigration law and to a movement (still percolating as of this writing) to declare California a "sanctuary state" that would resist the enforcement of just, constitutional, democratically enacted immigration laws. If that happens, perhaps the United States should sell California back to Mexico, for a symbolic price of one peso.

As California goes, so goes America, a decade or two later. The Daily Caller News Foundation reported,

> Children born to illegal immigrants, or "anchor babies" as they are sometimes called, become eligible to vote in U.S. elections once they turn 18. Though it is impossible to know the exact numbers, a DCNF analysis of estimates by the Pew Research Center demonstrates that over 1.6 million children of illegal immigrants are eligible to vote in U.S. elections, with over 5 million more becoming eligible to vote in the future....
>
> Most illegal immigrants are Hispanic or Asian, which are both heavily Democratic voting blocks. If the children of illegal immigrants hold similar voting patterns as their parents, it spells trouble for the GOP....
>
> "The broader point is that when you let lots of people into your country who are likely to vote for bigger government, it's going to change your politics, and even if we didn't have our current citizenship practices, you'd see the same thing happening just because of legal immigration," [Center for Immigration Studies executive director Mark] Krikorian said.[21]

What about Assimilation?

At this point, open-borders enthusiasts will point out that in past centuries the United States did import millions of people from backward, tyrannical parts of the world—ranging from starving Catholic Ireland to feudal

★ ★ ★

An Ally in the Effort for Smarter Immigration: The Center for Immigration Studies

The Center for Immigration Studies describes its position as "Low-immigration, Pro-immigrant." CIS seeks fewer immigrants but desires a warmer welcome for those admitted.

Founded in 1985, CIS has pursued a single mission: "providing immigration policymakers, the academic community, news media, and concerned citizens with reliable information about the social, economic, environmental, security, and fiscal con-sequences of legal and illegal immigration into the United States."[22] In other words, they crunch numbers and take the long, broad view.

CIS is naturally in the crosshairs of the Southern Poverty Law Center (SPLC), which makes a very rich . . . we mean VERY rich . . . business out of calling groups it opposes racists. In fact, the Center for Immigration Studies is a "SPLC-designated Hate Group."[23]

Southern Italy. Those people were assimilated successfully. Why can't we expect the same thing to happen now? This argument is logical on the surface, but in fact it is shallow and facile. The America of 2017 could hardly be more different from that of 1887 or even 1917. The migrants coming are different, both in the cultures from which they come, and the attitudes that they bring. The welcome they get is also radically different, as are the demands made of them. Our economy, laws, culture, and institutions have radically changed. Thus the same phenomenon, under extraordinarily new circumstances, has a very different impact. Imagine that. Will wonders never cease? Next thing you'll tell me that launching a war against Mexico or Canada—the United States did both in the nineteenth century—wouldn't play out the same way today.

Take any other political issue and try using the argument, "Well, we did it that way in 1840!" and see if people are persuaded. Liberals and radicals who otherwise scorn the argument from precedent—who demand that the Catholic Church ordain women and that the Supreme Court force

Evangelical bakers to celebrate the newly invented Constitutional right to gay marriage—suddenly become rabid traditionalists when the immigration issue comes up. Shouldn't that make us suspicious?

There are two appalling but stubborn realities that stand in the way of the United States benefiting (as it once did) from accepting large numbers of low-skill immigrants from very different cultural backgrounds. Take not one of them but both of them away, and then you might—just might—have a situation remotely comparable to the old America that once welcomed, assimilated, and profited from mass immigration. Leave either one in place, and you face catastrophe.

The Welfare State

The same liberals who in 1965 were championing radical changes to our immigration laws were also promoting the Great Society, which massively expanded the range, variety, and generosity of federal poverty programs. Thus even as they greatly expanded the number and variety of immigrants entering America, they removed one of the natural checks that had in the past protected America from the dangers of admitting too many people, or people with the wrong mindsets or skill sets. Namely, the free market. An immigrant who came to the United States in 1840, 1900, or even 1940 was expected to sink or swim. If he couldn't get work, or find affordable housing, or make peace with our political or legal system, there was no army of social workers, community organizers, and legal aid attorneys waiting to tell him that America was at fault—and provide him with economic support and legal redress. No, he faced the prospect of turning around and going home.

And millions did. While the Digital History project reports, "More Italians have migrated to the United States than any other Europeans," not all of them stayed. "The proportion returning to Italy varied between 11 percent and 73 percent," and overall "20 to 30 percent of Italian immigrants returned

to Italy permanently."[24] No doubt similar statistics could be cited for many other ethnic
groups who came before the explosion of the
welfare state. Today, those who arrive and find
no market for their labor can rely on a vast
array of government programs—which often
are sufficiently generous that they are more
appealing than the prospect of finding a job
back in the old country. That's especially true
for people who come to America from impoverished countries like Somalia, or chaotic ones like Mexico.

The America that once welcomed millions of newcomers was in one
sense a self-regulating mechanism: immigrants who thought that America
needed their labor but were mistaken would often return to their homes.
By creating a cradle-to-grave public welfare system, we have made America
a powerful magnet that draws poor people here and holds them tight. It
assimilates such immigrants not to the working and middle class world of
work that leads to self-respect and responsible citizenship but to the shadow
world of dependency, stagnation, hopelessness, and resentment. Meanwhile,
the constant influx of low-wage workers (legal and illegal) undermines the
economic prospects of low-skill workers born in the United States, making
it less likely that our native-born poor will ever escape the welfare trap.

The numbers are telling. In 2015, the Center for Immigration Studies (CIS)
documented the rates of public welfare use by immigrants, compared to non-
immigrant families. Here are some highlights excerpted from that report:

- In 2012, 51 percent of households headed by an immigrant
  (legal or illegal) reported that they used at least one welfare program during the year, compared to 30 percent of
  native households.

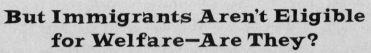

But Immigrants Aren't Eligible for Welfare—Are They?

"Most new legal immigrants are barred from welfare programs when they first arrive, and illegal immigrants are barred as well. But the ban applies to only some programs; most legal immigrants have been in the country long enough to qualify for at least some programs and the bar often does not apply to children; states often provide welfare to new immigrants on their own; naturalizing makes immigrants eligible for all programs; and, most important, immigrants (including illegal immigrants) can receive benefits on behalf of their U.S.-born children who are awarded U.S. citizenship at birth."
—the Center for Immigration Studies[25]

- Welfare use is high for both new arrivals and well-established immigrants. Of households headed by immigrants who have been in the country for more than two decades, 48 percent access welfare.
- Welfare use varies among immigrant groups. Households headed by immigrants from Central America and Mexico (73 percent), the Caribbean (51 percent), and Africa (48 percent) have the highest overall welfare use. Those from East Asia (32 percent), Europe (26 percent), and South Asia (17 percent) have the lowest.[26]

The social and political impact of importing millions of new Medicaid, welfare, and food stamp recipients each decade should be obvious: it undermines the American ideal of self-reliance and reliably boosts the political support for expanding such welfare programs. It strains the resources available for offering aid to native-born Americans who suffer injuries, become addicted, or lose their livelihoods thanks to technological or economic changes. It helps drive inequality in America by constantly growing the bottom tier of low-wage or no-wage Americans. It elects more left-wing Democrats, who in turn have every motive to expand immigration further.

It is also extremely expensive. CIS issued a follow-up study digging into the costs imposed on America of extending our safety net to millions of newcomers—who, unlike American citizens, didn't contribute to the system before collecting from it:

- The average household headed by an immigrant (legal or illegal) costs taxpayers $6,234 in federal welfare benefits....
- The average immigrant household consumes 33 percent more cash welfare, 57 percent more food assistance, and 44 percent more Medicaid dollars than the average native household....
- At $8,251, households headed by immigrants from Central America and Mexico have the highest welfare costs of any sending region—86 percent higher than the costs of native households.
- Illegal immigrant households cost an average of $5,692 (driven largely by the presence of U.S.-born children), while legal immigrant households cost $6,378.[27]

But wouldn't a border wall and the stricter enforcement of immigration laws (see chapter five) be even more expensive? Steven A. Camarota, the original researcher who turned up the shockingly high rate of welfare use by immigrants, decided to do the comparison. Relying on a National Academies of Sciences, Engineering, and Medicine (NAS) study, he calculated "a net fiscal drain of $74,722 per illegal crosser" but pointed out that that figure only covered "the original illegal immigrants and do not include any costs for their U.S.-born descendants. If we use the NAS projections that include the descendants, the fiscal drain for border-crossers grows to

$94,391 each." The wall, which is estimated to cost between $12 and $15 billion, would only have to prevent "160,000 to 200,000 illegal crossings (excluding descendants) in the next 10 years" in order to pay for itself. And that wouldn't be hard: "Newly released research by the Institute for Defense Analyses (IDA) done for the Department of Homeland Security indicates that 170,000 illegal immigrants crossed the border successfully without going through a port of entry in 2015.[3] While a significant decline in crossings from a decade ago, it still means that there may be 1.7 million successful crossings in the next decade. If a wall stopped just 9 to 12 percent of these crossings it would pay for itself. If a wall stopped half of those expected to successfully enter illegally without going through a port of entry at the southern border over the next 10 years, it would save taxpayers nearly $64 billion—several times the wall's cost."[28]

Multiculturalism and the End of Assimilation

So far the United States has been mostly spared the nightmare scenario Europe is living in: newcomers have taken over large swathes of major cities, where alien mores are enforced and women must conform to Middle Eastern standards of dress and behavior at the risk of violent sexual assault. Outside of some cities in Michigan, there are few places in America where a woman without a hijab would be menaced by haughty young men—who have plenty of time to harass people since they subsist on government benefits.

The reality of such "no-go" areas in places like Paris and Brussels has been hotly disputed by liberals, especially after candidate Trump made a reference to them on television. But journalists have verified that they are all too real. As the UK *Daily Mail* reported,

> French women who have been effectively banned from cafés and bars in certain 'no-go' suburbs in the country are fighting back.

Journalists and activists for TV channel France 2 went under-cover in various communities with high Islamic populations in Paris to show how conservative Muslim men are enforcing social segregation in public spaces....

The manager of one shop told them, "In this café, there is no mixing."

"We are in Sevran, not Paris. Here there is a different mental-ity. It is like back home," he added.

In Lyon, a city farther south, France 2 journalist Sinz spoke to a young woman who said she makes sure to be very careful in how she dresses.

She said she will often wear baggy clothes and no makeup to avoid being targeted by the Muslim men in the neighbourhood.

"I'm afraid, simple as that," she said, when asked why she feels she must alter her appearance.[29]

The next time you read a media account calling opponents of immigra-tion in France or other Western European countries "xenophobic" or "rac-ist," keep in mind the reality that they are facing: the full-scale invasion and occupation of their country by people who are intent on keeping their alien values intact and imposing them on others. Enabling or even encour-aging that is what leftists consider "acceptable," "mainstream" immigration policy. Opposing it is extremist.

What we face in America is not this total refusal to assimilate. Most immigrant children learn English, if not the Queen's English, or even William F. Buckley's. What they don't seem to be picking up—where would they?—is the rest of the cultural package that makes America work. As indicated by the statistics already cited here about reliance on public assistance, immigrant families today are not taking the path of hard work, self-reliance, independence, and upward mobility that reshaped previous generations of newcomers. Peter Skerry of the Brookings Institution observed that "immigrants and their children are assimilating—but not always to the best aspects of American society":

> Further evidence that English acquisition does not necessarily lead to the positive outcomes we expect, emerges from recent ethnographic research on the school performance of Latino adolescents. Several such studies report that although newly arrived students experience significant adjustment problems attributable to their rural backgrounds, inadequate schooling, and poor English-language skills, their typically positive attitudes contribute to relative academic success. Yet among Latino students born in the United States, the opposite is often the case. Despite fluency in English and familiarity with American schools, many such students are prone to adopt an adversarial stance toward school and a cynical anti-achievement ethic.... In the words of a veteran high school teacher, "As the Latino students become more American, they lose interest in their school work.... They become like the others, their attitudes change."[30]

Heather Mac Donald observes that the scarceness of entry-level jobs for young unskilled children of immigrants blocks off their movement into mainstream America, instead shunting them off into the same dead end that traps all too many African Americans:

> While Italian dropouts in 1904 could make their way into the middle class by working in the booming manufacturing sector or plying their existing craftsman skills, that is far more difficult today, given the decline of factory jobs and the rise of the knowledge-based economy. As the limited education of

Mexican-Americans depresses their wages, their sense of being stuck in an economic backwater breeds resentment. "The second generation becomes angry with America, as they see their fathers faltering," observes Cesar Barrios, an outreach worker for the Tepeyac Association, a social services agency for Mexicans in New York City. This resentment only increases the lure of underclass culture, with its rebellious rejection of conventional norms, according to Barrios.[31]

In a subsequent article, Mac Donald interviewed Jon Pederson, a pastor in an immigrant neighborhood in Santa Ana, California:

Participation in gangs and drug culture is rising in the second and third generation of Hispanic immigrants, he observes. "It's a perfect storm. When a family comes from Mexico, both parents need to work to survive; their ability to monitor their child's life is limited." Families take in boarders, often kin, who sometimes rape and impregnate the young daughters. "Daddy hunger" in girls raised by single mothers is expressed in promiscuity, Pederson says; the boys, meanwhile, channel their anger into gang life. Nearly 53 percent of all Hispanic births in California are now out of wedlock, and Hispanics have the highest teen birthrate of all ethnic groups.[32]

Teach Them to Resent America

Nor are our institutions encouraging these newcomers to adopt an identity as patriotic Americans. Schools that in the 1920s would have aggressively (perhaps even obnoxiously) striven to "Americanize" immigrants and their children now teach an America-bashing narrative that demonizes our Founders and even encourages aggressive foreign nationalism.

As far back as 1995, some California public schools were using a textbook that advocated the "reconquista" of the American Southwest by Mexico via mass immigration:

> Santa Barbara County has adopted a textbook which calls for the "liberation of Aztlan" by Chicanos. The book, *The Mexican American Heritage*, will be used for high school "Chicano studies" throughout Santa Barbara County.
>
> According to a review of the book by Debora L. Sutherland of Santa Barbara, the book introduces the concept of "Aztlan" in the first chapter and from that point on uses the term to mean the seven states of the Southwest which were ceded to the U.S. by Mexico in the Treaty of Guadalupe Hidalgo in 1848.
>
> "The book consistently questions the validity of our existing border with Mexico," Sutherland wrote. "It also makes it very clear that with the continuing influx of Latinos into the Southwest along with their high birthrate, these so-called 'natives' will realize their power to control Aztlan once again."[33]

Now such curricula have gone state-wide—which means, given the purchasing power of the California school system, that they will likely be imposed on dozens of other states. As Stanley Kurtz warned in *National Review* after reviewing the K–12 curriculum proposed for state-wide adoption in 2016, "I think it's fair to characterize California's new curriculum as openly anti-assimilationist.... the authors of the framework feel it necessary to insist that the ideal of immigrant assimilation is no longer appropriate, and was probably based on some combination of bigotry and selfishness when it flourished. The black power movement, with its demands for racial separatism and change 'by any means necessary,' is portrayed as beneficial, if misunderstood. The violent and still controversial American Indian

Movement gets similar treatment. Most striking of all, El Plan de Aztlan, the charter of the radical group MEChA, the militant separatist organization which aims to 'reconquer' the American Southwest for Mexico, is also featured as a benign example of sixties civil rights activism."[34]

Let's step back and tote up the differences between the experience of low-skill immigrants in, say, 1916 (the year John Zmirak's grandfather came to America from Austria-Hungary) and 2016. Back then, immigrants had to find work or go home. Today, immigrants can find enough government support that going home need not be an option. Immigrants then faced public institutions, schools, churches, and even employers who touted the benefits of "Americanization." Today they face institutions that say precisely the opposite. Immigrants like John's grandfather knew that they were privileged to be welcomed into America, and the institutions they interacted with reinforced the message. Immigrants and their children today are taught that they are victims. They enjoy affirmative action benefits (which were created for the descendants of slaves) at the expense of native-born white males. Their textbooks and teachers tell them that America exploited their ancestors, oppresses them now, and essentially owes them a living. What could go wrong?

Screwing America's Working Class

There's a final and very powerful reason to worry about mass low-skill immigration. Our current immigration status quo harms the most vulnerable Americans and serves the strong, the cozy, the comfortable. No doubt you've heard the argument that immigrants "do the jobs that Americans won't." It has the ring of good sense to it. We have all seen recent immigrants (legal and illegal) busting their butts at jobs which we might not want to do—busing tables in crowded diners, roofing houses in the hundred-degree Texas sun, disemboweling chickens in grim industrial slaughterhouses. We know that much of the agricultural work done in America's fields is performed by illegal immigrants. Increasingly, babies are tended while moms are at work, suburban houses are tidied, and yards kept mowed and watered, all by immigrant labor. Cheap-labor advocates warn us that without mass low-skill immigration, these jobs just wouldn't get done. Our fruit would rot in the fields and our lawns turn brown while our toddlers slowly starved in filthy, untended houses whose roofs leaked water year-round.

Weirdly, though, that wasn't what America looked like in 1965, the year that Ted Kennedy's immigration bill passed Congress and threw open the doors to massive low-skill immigration. In fact, the very jobs which we are told today are simply impossible for native-born Americans to perform were done by many of our parents. John Zmirak's father was a manual laborer, hauling mail on his back for the U.S. Postal Service for decades. His mother cleaned house and bused tables as a waitress. As late as the 1970s, teenaged Americans mowed their parents' lawns, and sometimes earned extra money doing the neighbors'. Babies got sat by high school girls. Low-wage entry level jobs were typically done by Americans, black and white, who might not have finished high school—so they put their strong backs and solid work ethics into "dirty jobs" that still offered decent salaries and allowed them to make a living. Working class wages grew steadily over the decades, and blue-collar jobs allowed poor men to become the heads of households, forming stable families.

A number of social changes, including the growth of the welfare state and the demands of toxic feminism, have helped to undermine those healthy realities. Foreign competition cut into many factory jobs. But there were and still are millions of blue-collar jobs that cannot be outsourced to Thailand or Malaysia—for instance, every single one that we just mentioned. But we "outsource" them to foreigners anyway, in the form of recent immigrants. The mass influx of cheap labor offered by eager immigrants has run down the wages for blue-collar jobs, cut off the bottom rungs of the ladder that was once used by poor Americans, and taught America's elites that it is somehow natural to have all the "grunt" jobs in society performed by poorly paid non-Americans. Labor unions, which once lobbied against mass immigration in order to protect their members' wages, have mostly been captured by social justice warriors and follow the lead of the only growing and powerful labor organizations—government employee unions, which benefit from importing new clients and voters for the administrative and welfare state.

Though labor leaders and even Democratic members of Congress from blue-collar districts ignore it, the law of supply and demand remains in effect. So does the law of entropy, which says that chaos tends to reign when you remove outside forces of order. The Democrats would deny both of those—and gravity, too, if it helped them get more votes.

Just as a massive gold-strike will lower the price of gold, a huge and sustained influx of low-skill labor will lower the price of labor. Harvard economist George Borjas, himself the son of immigrants, has run the numbers on the direct impact of immigration on wages:

> When the supply of workers goes up, the price that firms have to pay to hire workers goes down. Wage trends over the past half-century suggest that a 10 percent increase in the number of workers with a particular set of skills probably lowers the wage of that group by at least 3 percent. Even after the economy has fully adjusted, those skill groups that received the most immigrants will still offer lower pay relative to those that received fewer immigrants.
>
> Both low- and high-skilled natives are affected by the influx of immigrants. But because a disproportionate percentage of immigrants have few skills, it is low-skilled American workers, including many blacks and Hispanics, who have suffered most

from this wage dip. The monetary loss is sizable. The typical high school dropout earns about $25,000 annually. According to census data, immigrants admitted in the past two decades lacking a high school diploma have increased the size of the low-skilled workforce by roughly 25 percent. As a result, the earnings of this particularly vulnerable group dropped by between $800 and $1,500 each year.[35]

Yes, having more workers and consumers in an economy results in some economic growth. We wouldn't want to see zero immigration on the theory that this would raise the wages of everyone who is already here. But just because one extreme position is false, that doesn't make the opposite crackpot view any truer. Just as in the moral life we seek the golden mean, in public policy we seek the optimal outcome—the "sweet spot" which offers the most net benefits to those who need it most, with minimal harm. Anyone who thinks that the immigration status quo that prevails in America today really embodies that optimum has a very skewed set of values.

Again, we can thank Professor Borjas for taking this moral insight and quantifying it. As The Daily Caller reported on his testimony before the U.S. Senate in 2016:

> Based on a supply and demand model, Borjas found an increased supply of immigrants competing in the U.S. job market does produce a net gain for current U.S. workers of about $50 billion a year. But that small gain in the context of an $18 trillion economy is far outweighed by a transfer of wealth from U.S. workers to the businesses that hire those immigrants that amounts to $500 billion dollars.
>
> "What immigration really does is not so much increase the pie, as redistribute the wealth," Borjas testified before the Senate

Subcommittee on Immigration and the National Interest. "So what I've learned from all this is that immigration happens to come out to be just another government redistribution program."[36]

Except that this program, perversely, takes from the poor and gives to the rich, and hurts native Americans for the benefit of newcomers. It floods the labor markets that high school dropouts must compete in, for the benefit of the investors in corporations that profit from cheap labor. It provides affordable nannies for feminist activists and exotic restaurants for lobbyists. What it doesn't do is help the average American, whose taxes provide the social programs that such immigrants often need—since their employers offer few (or no) benefits.

The Only Really Bad Reason to Oppose Immigration

★ ★ ★
Dirty Jobs That Americans Will Do

The phrase "jobs Americans won't do" is dishonest on the face of it. To be truthful, it would need to be "jobs Americans won't do at current wages." Pay them enough, and Americans will do anything. They collect reeking garbage riddled with rats on the streets of ghetto neighborhoods. They work as unarmed guards in maximum security prisons. Some brave souls even teach in New York City public schools. They do that work because the wages are high enough to make it worth their while—and no one has yet figured out how to shoehorn poorly paid recent legal arrivals from Third World countries into those jobs. Give them time.

We've laid out here a long list of serious issues that drive millions of citizens to take seriously the need for gaining control over our country's borders, and limiting the number of low-skill immigrants we accept—especially from countries where cultural or religious norms are radically different from ours. There is another reason that some people oppose immigration—probably a small number, though there's no good way to measure it. That's because this opinion is taboo, the kind of thing you don't tell strangers taking surveys. Some people really do oppose immigration because they consider non-whites intrinsically inferior to white people and want to retain as much of a white racial majority in America as possible.

Let's talk about racism, shall we? In 2017, the host of The Alan Nathan Show asked John Zmirak why the Left flings reckless and groundless charges of racism at anyone who stands in the way of its policies, such as President Trump. John explained, "It's a way of trying to destroy someone, like falsely accusing him of rape or looking at kiddie porn," he said.

Our society's stigma against racist ideas and sentiments exists for a good reason. America still bears the scars of three hundred years of slavery and another hundred years of un-Constitutional segregation and bias. Our black fellow citizens deserve our special efforts to show equal respect and solicitude. Given that our own government (in the 1857 *Dred Scott* Supreme Court decision) specifically exempted black Americans from legal personhood and until 1964 allowed explicit and open racial discrimination, it seems reasonable that we bend over backwards for a while longer to root out the remnants of bias.

For that reason, our government reaches past what should be its proper powers and interferes with our freedom of contract and freedom of association to prevent us from abusing them to further racial discrimination. Given our government's past collusion with racism, this seems right for now. But that doesn't mean that the state should throw those freedoms in the garbage, as the Left is now demanding when it threatens to destroy Christian business owners for opting out of same-sex weddings.

Precisely because racism was the source of such appalling crimes, from the slave trade that shattered families to lynchings of black men with impunity right up through the Second World War, we ought not to trivialize the very word by flinging it far and wide when it doesn't apply. But that is precisely what leftists have learned to do, and it's a winning tactic. That's why they use it—not because they sincerely believe that it's "racist" for English literature departments to offer plenty of courses on great authors from England. Or for Americans to want their country's border to be controlled, just as Mexicans and Indians and Congolese want their countries' borders controlled.

Liberals aren't sincerely mistaken about the extent of racism in America. They are flat-out lying about it, cynically, to grab cultural power and terrorize their enemies. The abuse of the word "racism" is a nasty political smear, intended to tar people, especially those with conservative mores and a love for Western Civilization, with the blood that dripped from lynching trees in the unjust Jim Crow South.

The Left has even redefined the word "racism" to use it as a weapon. We now hear from campus authorities (this definition was promoted by the Obama DOJ civil rights division, if former officials J. Christian Adams and Christopher Coates are to be believed)[37] that only white people are capable of racism, because it is not essentially racial bias or hatred, but "privilege" connected with long-standing social dominance. If this sounds like Marxist gobbledygook, that's because it is. By this standard, when genocidal Hutus in Rwanda broadcast calls for the extermination of Tutsis, what they were doing wasn't racist—after all, the Tutsis had long been the "privileged" tribe. Nor is it racist when Syrian refugees torch a synagogue in Germany or campus leftists jeer at Jewish students and shout down Israeli speakers.

This handy repurposed slur is pretty much the ultimate insult. Our government explicitly tries to stamp out racism—with Ronald Reagan's support denying a tax exemption to a Christian school (Bob Jones University) when that school's policies seemed motivated by racial bias. Not just elites but ordinary people want to avoid the taint of racism, in part because of the stigma, but more because they know exactly how evil real racism is—from the extermination of Jews to the enslavement of Africans.

But not every accusation of racism is true. Those who lie on such serious subjects deserve contempt and consequences.

★ ★ ★

False Accusations

Sadly, false charges are used to discredit people all the time. Baseless accusations of child abuse are now a weapon in divorce custody battles, and campus feminists are demanding (and getting) kangaroo courts for sex disputes that trample the rights of the (often falsely) accused. Liberals tried to derail Betsy DeVos's nomination for secretary of Education, and smear a worthy free-speech group, the Foundation for Individual Rights in Education, for opposing those kangaroo courts. (And let's not forget *Rolling Stone*'s fake gang rape story, which nearly destroyed an innocent fraternity.)

Here's a safe rule in such cases: The more serious the charge, the more destructive it is if true, the higher the standard of evidence you should insist upon. And no one should get away with abusing our proper disgust at genuine racism, real child abuse, or the crime of rape in order to savage his political opponents.

So, of course, do genuine racists, who advance the arbitrary and groundless assertion that racial differences are so profound and consequential that they merit discrimination, segregation, and unequal treatment by the government. This claim is offensive on many levels. It flies against the bedrock American principle in the Declaration of Independence: that all men are created equal. It denies the universal human dignity that Western civilization learned from Christianity. It accepts pseudo-scientific theories like biological determinism, which reduces human beings to robots. Worst of all, it expresses contempt for millions of our fellow Americans, past and present, who worked (some slaved), fought, lived, and died as patriotic citizens. In simple justice (not even to mention charity) they deserve much better than that.

Given how genuinely noxious racism is, it's no surprise that leftists, open-borders utopians, multiculturalists, and cheap labor addicts want to smear everyone who opposes our corrupt and chaotic immigration status quo with this charge—pretty much the same way that defenders of segregation in the 1950s and '60s, and of Apartheid in South Africa, tried to tar all their opponents as Communists.

Now that we've laid out the problems of America's current immigration situation, it's time to find out how we got here.

CHAPTER TWO

The History of
Immigration in America

"America is a nation of immigrants." So people tell us, over and over and over again. It's a lovely, hypnotic mantra. It makes us...very sleepy. Suggestible. Ready to do whatever the mesmerist tells us to. But it's only partly true.

In the trivial sense, even the Native Americans were immigrants since their ancestors came from elsewhere. If mankind did indeed first appear in Africa, then every nation on earth outside that continent is a "nation of immigrants."

In the strict sense, the Europeans who settled America were not in any sense immigrants. They didn't come to a nation-state with a government and citizenship requesting the right to resettle. They didn't sneak across the border, either. They showed up, muskets in hand, and when they encountered mostly Stone Age hunter-gatherers, they traded with them, bought land, and fought until they conquered. (Just as the Indian tribes had been doing to each other for time immemorial.) We came first as settlers— more like the Vikings or the Visigoths than like huddled masses begging for refuge. You can call that a crime, or a human tragedy, or anything else you want. Except "immigration." That's the one thing it's not.

Did you know?

★ The Founders wanted to admit only immigrants who would make a net contribution and assimilate

★ At Ellis Island, immigrants were asked about the American flag and Constitution, plus where they planned to work

★ The percent of foreign-born in the United States today is the highest since World War I—and this time we're not doing "American-ization"

There was a period, from around 1848 until 1926, when the United States decided to accept large waves of immigrants. That reshaped us as a nation. But it doesn't oblige us to adopt such policies again unless they suit our national interest—as those policies did for eighty years or so.

What makes America different, unique, and especially valuable was in place long before the waves of European migrants landed on our shores. It was Anglo-American liberty, the fruit of the Magna Carta and countless subsequent struggles against centralized tyranny. English struggles, waged by the English people, in English, for English liberties.[1] Other countries that took lots of immigrants, such as Argentina, turned out very differently. And lands that till recently took very few non-Anglo immigrants, such as Australia, turned out much the same: free, prosperous, and comparatively orderly. Clearly immigration isn't the defining fact of America; ordered liberty is. If immigration begins to threaten that liberty—as you'll see that it has—it will have to be reined in. That is, if we wish to remain America in anything more than a pedantic, geographic sense.

A Nation of Assimilation

It's much more true, hence useful, to say that we are a nation of assimilation. At least that's what we aspire to. We aim to assimilate as many new people as is prudent to the values of ordered liberty that our ancestors fought to establish. Those who can't or won't sign on to that platform have no place among us. You will notice that neither of the authors of this book is named something like "Witherspoon" or "Wooster." Our ancestors came from nations with very different values, cultures, and political traditions from America's. They spoke different languages. They had non-American, even perhaps un-American civil habits. But they knew that they needed to adapt to their new environment and raise children who would live by their new country's rules. That was the price of freedom, social mobility, and all the other benefits that they had crossed the ocean to find. They paid the price, while those who couldn't or wouldn't, simply... went home. That's how it's supposed to work.

Our national motto is "E Pluribus Unum," or "From the Many, One." Define America not by assimilation but by immigration, and what you get is "From the Many, Many." That's not much of an achievement. And it won't yield a livable country, as we're grimly finding out. Without the unity of a coherent national culture with common mores, you don't have a nation at all. At worst you have civil war. At best you have an empire, yoked together despite all its divisions and mutual hatreds—its "diversity"—only by the power of the State. You know, like Rome. And empires don't have citizens. They have subjects, or even slaves.

Though America is more, far more, than a "nation of immigrants," the waves of settlement and then immigration that populated a sparsely settled continent certainly changed it. They influenced our culture and in many ways enriched it. They also posed serious challenges, which our ancestors confronted thoughtfully. Our forefathers didn't just sit back and pretend that immigration is a force of nature like sunspots, which we cannot control and must simply learn to live with. Immigration is a collection of policy decisions. We can have wise policies or foolish ones. We can take careful thought for the future, at the cost of being vilified in the present, or else we can duck and cover and let our descendants fend for themselves. To plan for the future, we must understand the past—the real past, not the air-brushed, sentimentalized, politically manipulative official story that multiculturalists with a lefty political agenda are feeding us.

The Four Great Waves of Immigration to America

Since independence, the United States has seen four major waves of immigration. It's worth a journey back to understand the nature of each. What gifts—and challenges—did those waves bring? What legitimate (and also what unfounded) concerns did each wave provoke among natives? What prudent steps did earlier generations of Americans take (or fail to take) to ensure that each of those influxes built the country up, instead of dividing it? Too often, historical accounts of immigration treat our ancestors like dopey music critics who panned Beethoven's symphonies or Chicken Little alarmists who were worried over nothing. In fact, each wave brought problems along with opportunities. If it weren't for careful policies—and occasional "nativist" pushback—those waves of immigration could have gone horribly wrong. You know, the way that our current mass influx of low-skill immigrants has.

Progressives with no respect for history but a gnawing hunger for power want to pretend that the United States really began in 1965. With Ted Kennedy's disastrous rewrite of our immigration laws.

What did our actual Founders have to say on immigration? Not the star of *Baywatch: Chappaquiddick*. We mean the ones who risked hanging for treason by King George in 1776. The answer might surprise you. It ought to chasten Democrats.

"The Harmony of Ingredients": The Founders Frame the Issue

As Wikipedia neutrally reports,

> The United States Constitution was adopted on September 17, 1787. Article I, section 8, clause 4 of the Constitution expressly gives the United States Congress the power to establish a uniform rule of naturalization.
>
> Pursuant to this power, Congress in 1790 passed the first naturalization law for the United States, the Naturalization Act

of 1790. The law enabled those who had resided in the country for two years and had kept their current state of residence for a year to apply for citizenship. However it restricted naturalization to "free white persons" of "good moral character."

The Naturalization Act of 1795 increased the residency requirement to five years residence and added a requirement to give a three years notice of intention to apply for citizenship, and the Naturalization Act of 1798 further increased the residency requirement to 14 years and required five years notice of intent to apply for citizenship. The Naturalization Act of 1802 replaced the 1798 Act.[2]

The cautious Benjamin Franklin was, in the words of David Bier at the Huffington Post, "by far the most vociferous critic of immigrants among the Founders." Franklin was worried about the "droves" of German migrants then settling into the Pennsylvania colony. In a 1751 book called *Observations Concerning the Increase of Mankind*, he asked, "Why should Pennsylvania, founded by the English, become a Colony of Aliens, who will shortly be so numerous as to Germanize us instead of our Anglifying them, and will never adopt our Language or Customs any more than they can acquire our Complexion?"[3]

In a letter two years later, Franklin was even more pessimistic: "Those who come hither are generally of the most ignorant Stupid Sort of their own Nation."[4] He complained that "[n]ot being used to Liberty, they know not how to make a modest use of it."[5] He even made reference to a claim that the Germans "are not esteemed men till they have shown their manhood by beating their mothers."[6]

Yet at the end of the day, Franklin still argued for what the new arrivals could bring to our shores. And his argument *for* immigration is even more telling than his argument against it. "I say I am not against the Admission of Germans in general, for they have their Virtues, their industry and frugality is exemplary," he wrote, "they are excellent husbandmen and contribute greatly to the improvement of a Country."[7] Notice the standards Franklin used. He didn't ask whether these newcomers had some inherent right to relocate to America. He didn't torture himself over whether he was indulging some anti-German bias. No, he pondered whether, on balance, they would contribute to the country. That is the same test that we should apply to immigration policy today.

Both the father of our country and the father of our Constitution shared a balanced view of immigration, as Michelle Malkin noted around the time Barack Obama usurped that Constitution in order to impose the DACA amnesty on the nation.[8] George Washington and James Madison, she noted, welcomed only those who could help the country—and would assimilate to its culture and political institutions:

James Madison was glad to have the "worthy part of mankind to come and settle amongst us, and throw their fortunes in common lot with ours." However, "Not merely to swell the catalogue of people. No, sir, it is to increase the wealth and strength of the community; and those who acquire the rights of citizenship, without adding to the strength or wealth of the community are not the people we are in want of."

This would exclude the immigrant who could not or would not, in Madison's words, "incorporate himself into our society."

And George Washington, as Malkin also points out, "in a letter to John Adams, similarly emphasized that immigrants should be absorbed into American life so that, 'by an intermixture with our people, they, or their descendants, get assimilated to our customs, measures, laws: in a word soon become one people.'"[9]

Ever practical, Washington would discourage immigration "except of useful mechanics and some particular description of men and professions."[10]

Yet his vision was not ungenerous. He said, "The bosom of America is open to receive not only the Opulent and respected Stranger, but the oppressed and persecuted of all Nations and Religions; whom we shall welcome to a participation of all our rights and privileges, if by decency and propriety of conduct they appear to merit the enjoyment."[11]

One early immigrant certainly came to "merit the enjoyment" of America. Not only did he become a Founding Father and our first secretary of the Treasury under the Constitution and get his face on the $10 bill. He ended up with his own smash Broadway musical.

That's right, Alexander Hamilton.

The cast of the Broadway musical that bears his name made a point of embarrassing Vice President-Elect Mike Pence, in part because of candidate Trump's immigration stance.[12] But Hamilton himself was cautious about the proper scale of immigration. Here's what he wrote in 1802: "The safety of a republic depends essentially on the energy of a common national sentiment; on a uniformity of principles and habits; on the exemption of the citizens from foreign bias and prejudice; and on that love of country which will almost invariably be found to be closely connected with birth, education, and family."

Hamilton further warned that "the United States have already felt the evils of incorporating a large number of foreigners into their national mass; by promoting in different classes different predilections in favor of particular foreign nations, and antipathies against others, it has served very much to divide the community and to distract our councils. It has been often likely to compromise the interests of our own country in favor of another."[13]

Somehow, that didn't make it into the musical.

So what was Hamilton's solution?

> The influx of foreigners must, therefore, tend to produce a heterogeneous compound; to change and corrupt the national spirit;

★ ★ ★

Our Founders' Creed

1. The purpose of immigration is building up the country, and nothing else.

2. It is entirely up to the citizens of the country to decide who and how many will join us.

3. We should welcome those who share the Anglo-American vision of liberty and will adhere to our Constitution.

4. We must reject those who cannot or will not do that.

5. The harmony of ingredients is all important.

to complicate and confound public opinion; to introduce foreign propensities.

In the composition of society, the harmony of the ingredients is all important, and whatever tends to a discordant intermixture must have an injurious tendency.[14]

With an attitude like that, would Hamilton be welcome at his own musical?

1776–1840: More of the Same

The first immigrants to build the American harmony were mostly Anglo, along with some Germans. They were almost exclusively white and Protestant. Just saying that nowadays, we feel like we should add some kind of apology. But we won't. It's just a fact, and nothing to be ashamed of. Indeed, given the dictatorships and oligarchies that cropped up in most non-Anglo countries of the New World, we ought to be grateful that our country was part of the Anglosphere. Of course, we are saddened by the ugly side of ethnic tribalism, and we are ashamed of slavery. But it existed in most other New World countries as well.

People with similar cultures, languages, and habits tend to stick together. Most Spaniards who went to the Americas relocated to places like Mexico or Argentina, which didn't encourage Anglo immigration— or even permit Protestant churches. Conversely, English-speaking

Protestants and others from northern European countries tended to settle in the United States or Canada. This fact helped create a cohesive culture in our new country, one that proved be far more tolerant of Jews, Catholics, and other religious minorities than most New World republics.

According to the 1790 census, about 80 percent of the white population of the United States was of British ancestry. Germans made up most of the other 20 percent. Many of them were very low-church Protestants, from long-persecuted sects that we now know as "Mennonite" or "Amish." "Pennsylvania Dutch" is a bastardization of *"Deutsch"*—the German word for "German." Of the 1790 U.S. population, a mere 2 percent were Roman Catholics, who still suffered some legal disabilities for a few decades, as the effects of the First Amendment gradually filtered down from the federal government into the states.[15]

Immigration to the United States started accelerating in the 1820s, with the number of new arrivals doubling to 143,000 by 1830 and then quadrupling in the next decade.[16]

What is vitally important to grasp is these new arrivals *closely matched the character* of our original founding populations. What's more, they reinforced the values that would turn a ragtag band of colonies into the most powerful nation in history.

★ ★ ★
Sticking Us with the Bill

It is worth noting that those who came here as indentured servants were not the responsibility of the fledgling republic, but of their employers. There were no government programs for which unsuccessful immigrants could apply, and on which they could become dependent.

This stands in stark contrast to our current situation: Big companies seek cheap labor, discourage immigration enforcement, and call for high totals of low-skill legal immigrants. When jobs dry up, those immigrants and their children become the responsibility of the taxpayer. That's where Democrat politicians come in, who see these migrant populations not so much as cheap labor but cheap votes.

A Book You're Not Supposed to Read

In his 1989 book *Albion's Seed: Four British Folkways in America*, published by Oxford University Press, historian David Hackett Fischer described four cultures (or "folkways") from distinct regions of Britain, and how those British cultural origins shaped the United States. Most of American history and culture before 1900, and even after, can be understood through the lens of these four waves of British settlers to America:

1. East Anglia to Massachusetts

Hard-working, thrifty, pious, and often censorious, these Protestants fled England to get away from the Anglican Church, which they saw as half-"papist," and likely to persecute them. It's to them that we owe the idea of America as a "City on a Hill," for better and worse. As the fierce Calvinism that had inspired the founding of colleges like Harvard, Yale, and Princeton faded into Unitarianism, the Puritan urge to form a "perfect" earthly community remained. On the bright side, New England produced some of America's most fervent abolitionists. New Englanders moved to the Midwest to open colleges such as Oberlin, which originally was a fervently Christian school that (almost uniquely) welcomed black students. But some people don't know when to stop "progressing."

Much of the Progressive movement, with its elitism and disdain for the grubby, stubborn fallenness of man, can be traced to degraded Puritanism. Ironically, the New England states are among the most "progressive" in the union. Even descendants from very different backgrounds, such as the Kennedys, assimilated to this post-Puritan worldview. In fact, as Vermont senator Bernie Sanders and his allies set the tone for the Democratic Party, and "intersectional" grievance activism becomes its own Puritanical religion, we can see that the much-mutated heirs of New England are politically very significant.

2. The South of England to Virginia

This culture helped form America as a nation, then mostly disappeared in the wake of the Civil War. It consisted of Englishmen who didn't much mind the Anglican Church, or social hierarchy, or landed aristocracy. They just wanted to move to the top of the pyramid. So they came to the richest colonies of the American South in pursuit of "huge tracts of land." They planted cotton, indigo, tobacco, and sugar, and at first relied on indentured servants to harvest it. When the supply volunteers for this cheap, hard labor began to dry up, they took advantage of the Slave Trade. That's how we ended up with apologists for liberty whose leisure depended on forced labor—like Thomas Jefferson.

There's no white-washing this fact. While the New England Puritans made plenty of money by trading slaves (Elihu Yale's donation that got the College named for him was partly funded by such profits), they didn't own many slaves themselves. That dirty job was subcontracted to Southern states. The infamous Constitutional compromise that only counted slaves as three-fifths of a person was something that the Northern states insisted on to avoid giving slave states more electoral votes and congressmen than their free populations merited. Today, states like California that oppose and sabotage immigration enforcement are awarded extra electoral votes and seats in Congress by a census that counts illegals as interchangeable with citizens. However, the financial and social strains of massive low-skill immigration are driving citizens out of such states, to the point where that phenomenon might just cancel out.

Many of the leaders of the American Revolution emerged from this culture, including George Washington, Patrick Henry, John Marshall, and other glittering names. We wince when we compare their eloquence on the subject of freedom with their lives as slave-owners, and there will always be some cognitive dissonance as we honor them. But without their fierce defense of free institutions against British administrative tyranny, America might not have gained its independence for decades, and it would have taken a very different shape.

The heirs to the Virginia Cavaliers, with their "damn the cost" embrace of cheap labor and blithe unconcern about social cohesion or equality, are surely Establishment Republicans such as Paul Ryan and the Bush clan.

3. North Midlands to the Delaware Valley

We often overlook the key contribution of Quakers and the states they shaped, especially Pennsylvania. But Friends who had fled intolerance in England helped to settle one of our most important states, which tellingly hosted the Continental Congress and the Constitutional Congress. Our nation's first capital was Philadelphia. Quakers urged peaceful co-existence with Indians and became important forces for the abolition of slavery. They also pioneered the creation of heavy industry in America, forming the core of our then-growing (and later dominant) merchant class. America's elite still likes to send its children to "Friends" schools, and to faintly Quaker colleges such as Haverford and Swarthmore. The earnest, straightforward, businesslike, and slightly naïve American Henry James pictured in his novels is the heir to the Quaker settlers' heritage. Think Jimmy Stewart, John Glenn, and Ronald Reagan.

Both political parties used to take their cue from this broadly American tradition. Richard Nixon and John F. (not Teddy) Kennedy tapped into this heritage. The vanishing American political center was heir to our Quaker forebears. But it has mostly disappeared, as "centrist" Democrats rush to the Left, pro-business Republicans take a Cavalier attitude toward massive demographic changes, and populist conservatives rally around the fourth and final wave of American settler culture…

4. Borderlands to the Backcountry

Here's where Trump's "Deplorables" got their start—among the fiercely independent, not always pious but revival-prone Scots-Irish who came to the United States from Ulster and Northern England. Known for clannishness, hostility to authority, distrust of government, and attachment to firearms, it was the Scots-Irish spirit that drove the settlement of the West, the independence of Texas, and most of our recent populist movements. Men like Andrew Jackson, Sam Houston, and Stonewall Jackson emerged from this culture. Today's heirs to this legacy would include Patrick Buchanan, Tucker Carlson, and most of the writers at Breitbart. Also Waylon Jennings, Merle Haggard, and Kinky Friedman.

It's no accident that the political party in the English-speaking world that is closest to the Republican party in its moral views is the Ulster Democratic Party, the one significant group in the United Kingdom that still opposes same-sex marriage and abortion. When Scots-Irish do get religion, it tends to be of the old-school, hard-shell biblical variety.

It's this unique hybrid of British folkways that permitted the survival of free institutions, religious pluralism, libertarian principles, and a vibrant economy. These cultural realities, much more than even the political principles debated at the Constitutional Convention, are what defined America.[17]

1840–1880: The Irish and the Germans (Two Different Recipes for Potatoes)

Immigration continued to accelerate in the mid-nineteenth century. This new wave consisted of mostly Western and Central Europeans, with large German and Irish contingents.

With cheap farmland and plentiful opportunity, the United States seemed an oasis to Germans fleeing the failed political revolutions of 1848, and the tiny plots of land in a crowded, splintered country. For the Irish,

America meant a matter of simple survival in the wake of the catastrophic Irish Potato Famine (1845–1849).[18]

The Irish tended to settle in the East while the Germans and Bohemians ventured to the Midwest.[19] This explains why kolaches seem as prevalent in Texas as cowboy boots. For that matter, that's how Texas's love affair with beer started. Writer Clay Coppedge put it this way: "The people who settled Texas were thirsty. They were thirsty when they got here and they have stayed thirsty. Since most of them came from Europe, they were thirsty for beer as much—or more—than anything else."[20]

Both the Germans and Irish were highly open to assimilating to America because of their negative experiences with aristocratic regimes, autocracy, and religious persecution back in Europe.

Religion and persecution would soon play a hand in their new land as well.

The first significant Catholic migration to America started in the mid-1840s. By 1850, Catholics made up about 10 percent of our population, a huge jump that provoked an often ugly but not entirely groundless reaction.

The Know Nothings

The arrival of large numbers of Roman Catholics triggered nativist anti-Catholic, anti-immigrant sentiments, seen most notably in the rise of the Know-Nothing Party. Party? It was more like a secret society. In fact, it started in 1949 as the secret Order of the Star-Spangled Banner, with lodges forming in nearly every major U.S. city.[21]

Eventually, this movement ventured into politics as the American Party or variants thereof. When members of local affiliates were asked for specifics about their organization, they would reply, "I know nothing." Critics soon dubbed them the "Know Nothings."

★ ★ ★

But One of These Things Is Not Like the Other

Unlike the Catholic teaching on religious persecution, which originated in the fourth century and was never taught "infallibly," Sharia law is a central pillar of Islam, and Muslim abuse of "unbelievers" goes back to the deeds of Muhammad himself.

The Know Nothings quickly gained in strength. By the end of 1855 they held forty-three seats in Congress.[22] Their hostility went beyond economic fears of newcomers competing for jobs. These "Know Nothings" were convinced that a "Romanist" (that is, papal) conspiracy was underway to undermine civil and religious liberty in the United States.

Their hostility often led to violence. Things exploded during the Kentucky governor's race in 1855. Fearful that Catholics were flooding the polls with non-citizens, and stoked by inflammatory rhetoric from the *Louisville Journal* editor George D. Prentice, local Know Nothings set out to stop them. On Monday, August 6—Bloody Monday—Protestant mobs attacked German and Irish Catholic neighborhoods. At least twenty-two people were murdered. Other incidents took place in Philadelphia and Massachusetts, including armed attacks on Catholic convents and churches.

Though the Know Nothings are rightfully condemned for their bigotry and violence, and thankfully they lasted as a serious political force for a mere four years, there was a seed of legitimacy to the Protestant concern over the influx of Catholics to the United States.

Our Founders were mostly low-Church Protestants. Their churches had been launched by reformers persecuted by Catholics. One of the most popular books in English for centuries was *Foxe's Book of Martyrs,* which listed the gruesome execution of pioneering English Protestants under Queen Mary I (Henry VIII's devoutly Catholic daughter).

As of the 1840s (and even the 1940s!) the Catholic Church preached that the persecution of Protestants by the government could be justified, at least in principle. Protestant churches and schools were banned through most of

Latin America, Spain, and the Papal States, as they had been for centuries, and would be in Spain through the 1970s. (Pope John Paul II officially apologized for such persecution in January 1999.)[23] So on the surface, Know-Nothing worries about Catholic immigration may have been reasonable—along the lines of current fears about the influx of Muslims who accept Sharia law, which demands the subjugation of "infidels" worldwide.

But in fact, contrary to the notions of the Know Nothings, U.S. bishops rejected religious persecution and embraced the American system. So did virtually all American Catholic immigrants, many of whom were coming from lands where official churches (Catholic and Protestant) enjoyed wide privileges at the expense of ordinary citizens and religious dissenters. They wanted no part of any organized intolerance or established Church. So hostile were American Catholics to the official theory of religious intolerance that Pope Leo XIII warned against a possible "Americanist" heresy.[24] The Church would finally embrace religious liberty for all at Vatican II in 1964, in part thanks to the lobbying of American bishops such as Francis Spellman of New York.

Foreswearing Foreign Princes

One concession to anti-Catholic fears was, as we have seen, the revision of the U.S. citizenship oath to include renouncing political allegiance to "foreign princes" (that is, the pope). Our ancestors gladly took it, and Catholics have always kept it. Perhaps in lieu of a Muslim ban, the citizenship oath needs another update, to include foreswearing allegiance to any religious code that advocates religious persecution, the oppression of women, and replacement of the U.S. Constitution with Sharia law.

The Irish Problem

If nativists were wrong to worry that the Irish brought the seeds of theocracy with them, in fact they brought plenty of other real problems. John Zmirak told the story in *The Bad Catholic's Guide to Wine, Whiskey & Song*, noting that the Irish "once appeared to Americans as a menace to public order and democracy—and not just once a year, during the St. Patrick's Day Parade":

> From the 1820s on through the 1870s, thousands of Irishmen sailed annually to escape the repression and poverty imposed upon the Irish by the English. As William Stern wrote in a famous *City Journal* article,[25] in occupied Ireland, Catholics were

>> barred from ever owning a house worth more than five pounds or holding a commission in the army or navy. Catholics could neither run schools nor give their children a Catholic education. Priests had to be licensed by the government, which allowed only a few in the country. Any Catholic son could seize his father's property by becoming a Protestant.

> Even the slums of New York and Boston sounded promising by comparison. As Irish climbed out of steerage and "coffin ships," they raised suspicions on the part of natives and nativists—who feared the influx into a pristinely Protestant America of millions of loyal 'papists.'
>
> Prominent Americans from John Quincy Adams to John Calhoun asked aloud if these ragged emigrants were the vanguard of 'Romish tyranny.' To make matters worse, when the Potato Famine devastated Ireland in the 1840s, the influx became a torrent—and the immigrants arrived in an appalling condition. As Stern described the new arrivals:

>> In New York they took up residence in homes intended for single families, which were subdivided into tiny

apartments. Cellars became dwellings, as did attics three feet high, without sunlight or ventilation, where whole families slept in one bed. Shanties sprang up in alleys. Without running water, cleanliness was impossible; sewage piled up in backyard privies, and rats abounded. Cholera broke out constantly in Irish wards. Observers have noted that no Americans before or since have lived in worse conditions than the New York Irish of the mid-nineteenth century.

Illiteracy, alcoholism, and prostitution were rampant. Irish indeed formed America's first underclass—and set some natives (such as the anti-Catholic cartoonist Thomas Nast) wondering whether they were some inferior sub-species of *homo sapiens.*

What saved the Irish from this desperate situation, as Stern documents, was neither a government program nor a guerilla movement. Instead it was the efforts of the local Catholic Church, led by the intrepid and bellicose Archbishop 'Dagger' John Hughes....

Hughes fought poverty through compassion. And not the nanny state, non-judgmental kind which nowadays hands out condoms to schoolkids and free needles to addicts. Hughes used his parishes to start a chain of Catholic schools which would drill the ragamuffin children of recently-starving laborers in useful trades and the catechism, and universities such as Fordham to teach the liberal arts. At their churches, his pastors preached purity and penance. They'd dispense food and clothes to needy workmen—but only after sniffing their breath for the scent of whiskey. Young women who wanted the nuns to find them work had to keep a blameless good name. Orphans and the sick could find shelter in Church-run homes.

Soon, the once-destitute Irish re-formed themselves into a healthy working class. As Stern documents, the tough love of good priests like Hughes, and the nuns who staffed their schools, in a single generation pulled an entire people out of penury—and into the NYPD.[26]

The Asians: Hard Work in the Face of Groundless Hostility

Meanwhile on the West Coast, another group of immigrants was beginning to make America their home: immigrants from Asia. They weren't looking for a land of milk and honey. They were looking for gold! The California Gold Rush ignited a mad scramble to the West, which it would be downright rude to call a "Chinese fire drill." And that wouldn't be fair. Thousands of white Americans also dropped everything and came in search of quick riches. But the Asian numbers are fascinating. In 1848, Chinese immigrants on the West Coast numbered fewer than four hundred. By 1852, there were twenty-five thousand.[27] They weren't just prospectors. Laborers and merchants came as well, realizing that all those miner 49ers needed somewhere to buy their equipment and spend their nuggets.

Like the Irish and Germans before them, the Chinese and other East Asian arrivals faced hostility. Racism certainly played a part. Nativists issued apocalyptic warnings of a "yellow peril,"[28] of hordes of Genghis Khan–like conquerors coming to subjugate America.

But there were other factors beyond blind Sinophobia.

1. Employers used the new arrivals to drive down wages.[29] Thankfully, companies today would never, ever use cheap, unskilled immigrant labor to drive down the wages of citizens. Right?

2. Employers used Chinese workers as a weapon against the growing organized labor movement.[30] *You want to form a union? I've got a boatload of Chinese waiting to take your place.*

3. Finally, and most significantly, these immigrants were, in fact, from an entirely different culture; one could say an "alien" culture. More particularly, a culture that had no tradition of liberty.

How could these exotic Asian ingredients ever hope to harmonize with the Irish, British, and Western Europe stew (served up in a bowl of strictly white bread)?

It wouldn't prove easy, and the federal government certainly went out of its way to make it difficult.

In 1882, President Chester Arthur signed into law the Chinese Exclusion Act. No fancy euphemism to hide that law's intent! It did what it said. It banned the immigration of Chinese laborers. And then it made sure to define laborers as broadly as possible. The Chinese Exclusion Act would be the first significant federal legislation restricting immigration.

For the first time, Federal law proscribed the entry of an ethnic working group on the premise that their admission endangered the good order of certain localities.[31] The concern was purely race-based; no other race or nationality faced the same restriction.[32] Ever. Still, the Supreme Court upheld the Act. And the court was correct. Congress has every right to pass laws, even bad laws, regarding the acceptance of foreigners into America. We can exclude or include them arbitrarily.

Still, the Chinese in the United States fought hard to assimilate, to serve, to make their way in their new home. Most legitimately. Even nobly, given widespread lynchings, discrimination, and harassment. Despite all this, the vast opportunities offered them in a growing, dynamic country stood in stark contrast to the chaos of late Manchu China, not to mention the

A Book You're Not Supposed to Read

The Irish Way: Becoming American in the Multiethnic City by James Barrett (Penguin Books, 2012).

genocide suffered by Chinese at the hands of Japanese occupiers; the staggering horror of Mao's Communist regime, which claimed (a middle estimate) some thirty-five million people;[33] and finally China's brutal One Child policy that forced millions of abortions and caused a "gendercide" of millions of baby girls. Contemporary China still persecutes Tibetans, Uighur Muslims, and other minorities. Discrimination comes in all colors.

It would be 1943 before Congress repealed the Chinese Exclusion Act and allowed Chinese-born citizens to naturalize. In June of 2012, Congress unanimously passed a bipartisan resolution formally regretting the Chinese Exclusion Act.[34] The resolution was introduced by U.S. Congresswoman Judy Chu…the daughter of Chinese immigrants.

1880–1926: Italians and East Europeans Are Americanized

One day in 1916 the young fisherman Patrick Zmirak left Zagreb, Austria-Hungary, and set out for America. To gain admission to the United States, he joined its Merchant Marine and served on American ships in U-boat infested waters. When the war ended, he settled in Hell's Kitchen, Manhattan, attending the Croatian-language parish of Saints Cyril and Methodius. He worked for the rest of his life shoveling coal into the engines of tugboats on the East River. His son, John Patrick Zmirak, would be schooled by the Irish Christian Brothers of Sacred Heart Parish and serve under George Patton in the Sixth Cavalry in the occupation of Germany. Then he'd come home to become a letter carrier. His son, John Patrick Zmirak Jr., would go to Yale and become an author.

Augustine Perrotta and his bride Concetta arrived from Italy. He was a silk weaver by trade and a professional musician. The Perrottas settled in Paterson, New Jersey. During World War II, Democrat President Franklin Delano Roosevelt would order Augustine Perrotta's radio (and those of other Italian immigrants) confiscated over slanderous fears they might be serving as spies for Mussolini. This as his son was serving in the Army overseas. That son would become one of the original Singing Sergeants and spend his career with the United States Air Force Band.

A few miles away, in Haledon, New Jersey, Julius Pellegrino, originally of Naples, Italy, had opened a liquor store. One son would build the family business. Another would race to enlist in the U.S. Navy after Pearl Harbor, then build planes with Howard Hughes. Both brothers achieved the American Dream.

Julius's elder daughter married a construction contractor and worked at Quackenbush Department Store in Paterson. Younger daughter Helen stopped by Quackenbush one day on her way to business school. In America a woman could go into business. But she took one look at Augustine Perrotta's son Al hard at work in the store, and said, "That's for me." She got herself a job at Quackenbush that very day. Al's heart never had a chance. And after World War II, the daughter and son of Italian immigrants brought a quartet of Americans into the world.

All four of their children would serve the U.S. military in one capacity or another. The youngest, Al Perrotta, would become a writer (though wishing he was a musician like his dad and grandpa).

The Zmiraks and Perrottas provide but two of the millions upon millions of unique stories that made up the next and most epic wave of immigration to the United States. It was this wave that inspired Emma Lazarus's beautiful poem, which sits on a plaque at the museum on Liberty Island.

"The New Colossus" by Emma Lazarus

Not like the brazen giant of Greek
    fame,
With conquering limbs astride from
    land to land;
Here at our sea-washed, sunset gates
    shall stand
A mighty woman with a torch, whose
    flame
Is the imprisoned lightning, and her
    name
Mother of Exiles. From her beacon-
    hand
Glows world-wide welcome; her mild
    eyes command
The air-bridged harbor that twin cities
    frame.
"Keep, ancient lands, your storied
    pomp!" cries she
With silent lips. "Give me your tired,
    your poor,
Your huddled masses yearning to
    breathe free,
The wretched refuse of your teeming
    shore.
Send these, the homeless, tempest-
    tost to me,
I lift my lamp beside the golden door!"

Mostly this sea of humanity hailed from Eastern and Southern Europe. After 1892 they would pass through, and be processed, at the nation's first federal immigration station: Ellis Island.

Ellis Island

Ellis Island, located in the shadow of the Statue of Liberty, was no mere pit stop. Getting into America took more than hopping off the boat. Before your boat even left the Old Country, you would have to answer a twenty-nine-question questionnaire as part of a ship's manifest log.[35]

That document was used by inspectors at Ellis Island to cross-examine the immigrant. The examination took place in the Registry Room, also known as the Great Hall. Arrivals were also given a physical.

According to the Statue of Liberty–Ellis Island Foundation, only 2 percent of arriving immigrants were excluded from entry: "The two main reasons why an immigrant would be excluded were if a doctor diagnosed that the immigrant had a contagious disease that would endanger the public health or if a legal inspector thought the immigrant was likely to become a public charge or an illegal contract laborer."[36]

Imagine if we applied those standards today. First, do we have any idea how many of the twelve million or so illegal immigrants in this country are carrying

★ ★ ★

The Ellis Island Immigration Quiz

What is your name?

How old are you?

Are you male or female?

Are you married or single?

What is your occupation?

Are you able to read and write?

What country are you from?

What is your race?

What is the name and address of a relative from your native country?

What is your final destination in America?

Who paid for your passage?

How much money do you have with you?

Have you been to America before?

Are you meeting a relative here in America? Who?

Have you been in a prison, almshouse, or institution for care of the insane?

Are you a polygamist? Are you an anarchist?

Are you coming to America for a job? Where will you work?

What is the condition of your health?

Are you deformed or crippled?

How tall are you?

What color are your eyes/hair?

Do you have any identifying marks? (scars, birthmarks, tattoos)

Where were you born? (list country and city)

Who was the first President of America?

What are the colors of our flag?

How many stripes are on our flag? How many stars?

What is the 4th of July?

What is the Constitution?

contagious diseases? Are we supposed to just grin and bear it when illnesses that have no history in America start showing up in clusters with heavy immigrant populations? When people with no means or insurance fill up the emergency wards of our public and private hospitals? (In case you're wondering why paying patients are charged $10 for Q-Tips®, there's the reason.) It's kind of funny to think that the same people who want an open border won't even grab a shopping cart without using hand sanitizer.

Notice the underlying themes behind the questions immigrants were asked: *Do you have a job lined up? Do you have skills? Do you have any money? Do you have a basic understanding and appreciation for the United States?* The concerns behind the questionnaire are the same ones that animated Ben Franklin and George Washington's concerns over immigration, and that conservatives still worry about today: *Will newcomers be burdens or blessings? Are they looking for opportunities or entitlements?*

Still, only 2 percent were rejected.

For the 98 percent who made it through inspection, their time at Ellis Island was short. In some three or four hours they were free to start their new lives in America.

Who were they?

These immigrants were culturally even further from the original American mix than the Irish had been. They came from lands with no traditions of self-government and often brought with them radical notions that had become popular in their home countries among unhappy, oppressed minorities. This included anarchist and radical socialist ideas popular in Russia, Germany, and Italy. It would be the anarchist son of an immigrant, Leon Czolgosz, who assassinated President William McKinley in 1901.[37]

Americanization

To counter such radical movements and to promote Hamilton's "harmony of ingredients," in the nineteen-teens the nation launched both formal and informal "Americanization" efforts. The idea was to move immigrants into absorbing American values, beliefs, and customs.

Key to the effort was learning the English language and American civics. We don't mean the kind of civics lesson popular today, which paints our Founders primarily as oppressors and America as a predator regime with a flawed Constitution. Quite the contrary. If anything, the picture that newcomers were given of the United States was overly sunny and upbeat. But then they were primed to think the best of a new country that offered them endless opportunities compared with the lands from which they came. Local governments, churches, and even employers set up "Americanization Schools" that immigrants eagerly attended to speed up their full participation in the experiment that is America.

But much of the heavy lifting was done just in the process of having to live and interact with Americans. As historian James Barrett has written, "A key to understanding the multi-ethnic American city is that most immigrants came to understand their new world less through such formal programs, than through informal contacts with the Irish and other experienced working-class Americans of diverse ethnic backgrounds in the streets, churches, and theaters."[38]

Scholar John F. McClymer notes that the Americanization movement climaxed during World War I as eligible young immigrant men were drafted into the Army and the nation made every effort to integrate the European ethnic groups into the national identity. Italian-born immigrants sent their sons to war, bought war bonds, and set up shops and restaurants and other small businesses.[39]

Mothers were the target of Americanization efforts among Mexican immigrants because of the strong influence they had on their sons. There was a strong effort to Americanize young Mexican girls, since they would be mothers likely to influence both home and community.[40]

The aggressive "Americanization" campaigns mostly succeeded. Millions upon millions of proud Americans were the result. The blessing on our land is immeasurable. The Melting Pot was getting tastier by the moment.

But it was about to boil over. The issues with anarchists and communists (including a series of bombings in 1919), the success of socialist revolutions in Europe, the sheer volume of new arrivals, and a desire to tighten the labor supply and raise wages, all contributed to calls in the 1920s for restrictions on immigration. Also at play was a movement that rejected the American Melting Pot…as a matter of "science."

The Progressives, Eugenics, and the Fantasy of Ethnic Purity

A 1921 *New York Times* article gives you some of the flavor of a new movement—left-wing and elitist—that rejected immigration:

> Severe restriction of immigration is essential to prevent the deterioration of American civilization, according to students of race and biology now taking part in the Second International Eugenics Congress at the American Museum of Natural History.
>
> The "melting pot" theory is a complete fallacy, according to eugenicists, because it suggests that impurities and baser qualities are eliminated by the intermingling of races, whereas they are as likely to be increased, if not more likely to increase.[41]

Progressive icon Woodrow Wilson helped kick-start the eugenics movement. President Wilson was, as Paul Rahe has described him, "a champion of eugenics and racial pseudo-science." His prejudice against blacks is well documented; under his leadership, segregation in the civic service would become law.[42] (Yet for some reason nobody is talking about renaming the Wilson Bridge on the Washington Beltway.)

Wilson said that the U.S. government was "accountable to Darwin, not to Newton." The Declaration of Independence and the Constitution were out of date—along with the limitations on the power of the presidency, which Wilson resented and did his best to evade.

In the midst of World War I, when countless immigrants were fighting and dying for the United States, Wilson pushed for the Sedition Act of 1918 to rid the land of political undesirables. According to law professor David D. Cole, Wilson's "federal government consistently targeted alien radicals,

★ ★ ★

Demagogue-in-Chief

In a 1915 speech credited with helping set the stage for anti-immigrant hysteria, Wilson decried those immigrants "born under other flags" who have "poured the poison of disloyalty in the very arteries of our national life" and who "debase our politics to the uses of foreign intrigue." Oh, the number is not as great as those who have "enriched" our land, "but it is great enough to have brought deep disgrace upon us" and required laws "by which we may be purged of their corrupt distempers."[43]

deporting them...for their speech or associations, making little effort to distinguish terrorists from ideological dissidents."[44]

Purging immigrants was just part of the plan. The eugenicists' racist views gave rise to Margaret Sanger's Birth Control League, which would campaign successfully in thirteen states for the mandatory sterilization and even castration of those who failed culturally biased IQ tests. Stopping undesirables from entering our ports wasn't enough. These Progressives didn't even want them entering the world.

The Immigration Act of 1924

In 1921 Congress passed the Emergency Quota Act, which restricted the number of immigrants admitted from any country annually to 3 percent of the number of residents from that same country that had already been living in the United States as of the U.S. Census of 1910. This act set out two principles for immigration restriction: not just how many people could come into the United States, but who. These new limits came to be known as the National Origins Formula.[45]

The temporary Emergency Quota Act was made permanent by the Immigration Act of 1924, which reduced the quota to a mere 2 percent based on the 1890 census.[46]

This heavily weighed the scales towards Northern Europeans, and against Southern and Eastern Europeans, particularly Eastern European Jews. The goal was to freeze in place an Anglo, Northern European culture that seemed to be working, and to keep out the cultures of countries that were tearing themselves apart (such as Russia, Italy, and Mexico.) The idea, says the State Department Office of the Historian, was "to preserve the ideal of American homogeneity."

Not all of this can be traced to crank eugenics. Remember that the very borders of countries in Europe had just been redrawn at the Treaty of Versailles to diminish the perceived cause of ethnic hostility: "incompatible" groups unwilling to live together under the same government. The flaw in this ethnic resettlement—in the form of large German minorities orphaned in new weak states, would be exploited by Hitler to carve up and swallow neighboring countries. In fact, everyone took nationality a little too seriously back then, not just WASPy Americans.

The 1924 Immigration Act also completely excluded Arabs and Asians. The Japanese were particularly angry, as the law shattered the so-called Gentleman's Agreement between the United States and Japan. But, as the State Department's website puts it, "Despite the increased tensions, it appeared that the U.S. Congress had decided that preserving the racial composition of the country was more important than promoting good ties with Japan."[47] And how did that one work out for us?

The numbers demonstrate the effect of the 1924 Act: to take one example, while immigration from Great Britain and Ireland fell 19 percent, immigration from Italy plummeted more than 90 percent.[48] The new quotas were so severe that, according to a study by Steven G. Koven and Frank Götzke, in 1924 there were more Italians, Czechs, Yugoslavs, Greeks, Lithuanians,

Hungarians, Portuguese, Romanians, Spaniards, Jews, Chinese, and Japanese leaving the United States than arriving as immigrants.[49]

Bad Rationale, Prudent Policy

The system set up by the Immigration Act of 1924 is now universally condemned by right-thinking people. But…however politically incorrect it may be to say it, the bill did its job in at least one sense.

It provided a much-needed "pause," allowing America to assimilate a massive, historic wave of migrants. As the years passed they intermarried with Americans of different ethnicities from their own, joined the Army, the Rotary Club, and the PTA. They became real Americans. And unlike so many other developed countries, America did manage to weather the Great Depression without producing any large-scale totalitarian movements of Left or Right. In fact, the same America that used ethnic quotas to restrict immigration in 1924 would, within a generation, defeat the racist regimes of Germany and Japan—albeit with a segregated military, thanks to Woodrow Wilson.

1965 to the Present: Mass Low-Skill Migration

For more than forty years, America's immigration policy remained virtually unchanged. In that time, the United States managed to overcome a Depression, win a World War, enjoy huge economic and technological development, outlaw segregation, begin conquering of space, and invent rock-n-roll, the hot rod, and the hula-hoop.

But then, captivated by Dr. Martin Luther King's vision of a nation where people were judged not by the color of their skin but by the content of their character, the nation looked at its immigration restrictions and found them lacking. Sadly, the law that came to replace the 1924 act was based more on fuzzy sentiment than cold, empirical reality.

In 1965, the Immigration and Nationality Act completely overhauled—or undid—the rules for who was allowed to immigrate to the country. Its major provisions:

- Abolished the quota system, the National Origins Formula
- Limited immigration from the Western Hemisphere for the first time
- Established a new immigration policy giving priority to uniting immigrant families. Seventy-four percent of visas would be designated for that purpose

★ ★ ★

Bad Timing

The 1965 Act has resulted in a massive restructuring of our nation's make-up, heavily weighted toward low-skill migrants from countries with large extended families—during just the time when our nation's manufacturing base was emigrating to lower-wage countries. It also introduced dozens of new languages, different cultures, and intractable un-American worldviews into our nation's bloodstream—at precisely the same time that multiculturalism and other leftist movements were challenging the very idea of assimilation, or asserting that America is fundamentally flawed, and not worth assimilating to.

When it was passed, its supporters insisted the Act would do little to change our nation, arguing that the Act was more a recognition of a moral principle.[50] They were either completely deluded, or else they were lying. President Lyndon B. Johnson claimed that the Act was "not a revolutionary bill. It does not affect the lives of millions.... It will not reshape the structure of our daily lives or add importantly to either our wealth or our power." Senator Ted Kennedy was a leading mover on the Act. Here's what he had to say:

First, our cities will not be flooded with a million immigrants annually. Under the proposed bill, the present level of immigration remains substantially the same...

Secondly, the ethnic mix of this country will not be upset.... Contrary to the charges in some quarters, [the bill] will not inundate America with immigrants from any one country or area, or the most populated and deprived nations of Africa and Asia....

In the final analysis, the ethnic pattern of immigration under the proposed measure is not expected to change as sharply as the critics seem to think.... The bill will not flood our cities with immigrants. It will not upset the ethnic mix of our society. It will not relax the standards of admission. It will not cause American workers to lose their jobs.[51]

Well, that turned out to be about as true as his original stories about Mary Jo Kopechne.

In the Act's first three decades, more than eighteen million legal immigrants flooded into the United States—more than three times as many as had been admitted in the previous three decades.[52] Today we allow a million more aliens a year to enter legally, to say nothing of the eleven to twenty million illegal aliens "in the shadows," in our hospitals, schools, welfare offices... or packing campaign rallies for Democrats.

Between 1965 and 2000, the highest number of immigrants (4.3 million) to the United States came from Mexico, in addition to some 1.4 million from the Philippines. Korea, the Dominican Republic, India, Cuba, and Vietnam were also leading sources of immigrants, each sending between seven and eight hundred thousand over this period.[53] But Mexico was responsible for three times as many new legal immigrants as any other nation on the face of the planet.

Between the 2008 recession and February 2015, the total net employment gains in the United States went to foreign-born workers, while native born workers suffered net job loss. The foreign-born gained 1.9 million jobs; native-born lost 1.1 million.[54]

All told, Uncle Teddy did a number on Uncle Sam.

Chain Migration

A particularly problematic result of the new 1965 immigration regime was "chain migration." While the bill set numerical restrictions on visas at 170,000 per year, with a per-country-of-origin quota, there were no limits on the number of immediate relatives of U.S. citizens and "special immigrants."[55] So an immigrant settles and gets citizenship, and now his family gets jumped to the front of the line. This in a nation where we don't even like it when someone is allowed to cut in line at a grocery store.

Chain migration means that no grant of amnesty (to DACA, or Dreamers, or the next handy acronym full of illegal immigrants) is a one-time measure of mercy. Instead it's the tip of a huge, theoretically infinite iceberg.

Every one of these amnestied illegals would be eligible to "sponsor" his extended family into the United States. As NumbersUSA explains:

> Chain Migration refers to the endless chains of foreign nationals who are allowed to immigrate to the United States because citizens and lawful permanent residents are allowed to sponsor their non-nuclear family members.
>
> It is the primary mechanism that has caused legal immigration in the U.S. to quadruple from about 250,000 per year in the 1950s and 1960s to more than 1 million annually since 1990.[56]

"Chain" migrants get in not because of their skills. Or education. Or experience. Nor for any other rational criterion. They just benefit from immigration nepotism. That got enshrined in law by Senator Ted Kennedy in 1965. It pleased his Irish constituents in Massachusetts.

The 1986 Amnesty amplified the problem. The Federation for American Immigration Reform (FAIR) has noted that "illegal aliens given amnesty by Congress in 1986 are now fueling naturalization in record numbers. As these former illegal aliens become citizens, all of their immediate relatives qualify to come immediately to the United States, and start new migration chains of their own."[57]

So for every Dreamer the Democrats want President Trump to amnesty, remember this: there may be four, six, eight, ten, or more new immigrants coming into the country on his invitation. And once they're here *they* get to hand out invitations. The fun never has to end, till the country does.

Americans reject chain migration. In a 2018 article, LifeZette reports:

> A new poll has found that Americans overwhelmingly favor curtailing "chain migration."...The survey, commissioned by NumbersUSA and conducted by Pulse Opinion Research just before Christmas, had a 3 percent margin of error.
>
> Some 57 percent of likely midterm voters favored ending the ability of new citizens to sponsor extended family members for immigration if Congress offers a path to citizenship for young adult illegal immigrants. Some 32 percent said they support continued chain migration.[58]

★ ★ ★

Only as Strong as Its Weakest Link

These chain migrants often come from troubled countries. Or bring with them dangerous ideas. In December 2017, Bangladeshi immigrant Akayed Ullah was offended by U.S. attacks on ISIS—and by the Christmas decorations in Times Square. So he blew off his genitals trying to set off a bomb in New York City. Ullah was the nephew of an American citizen. That uncle came to the United States under our pointless "diversity lottery." Ullah came via "extended family chain migration." See how this works?[59]

What's more, the new arrivals overwhelmingly tend to vote liberal and pro-choice. The millions of future Democrats that "Dreamer" illegals amnestied by DACA could invite here in future decades would make their mark. They'd seal the fate of the Republican party nationally. They'd turn states like Texas purple, then blue. We might never have another pro-life president again.

★ ★ ★

Another Ally in the Effort for Smarter Immigration: The Federation for American Immigration Reform

"The mission of the Federation for American Immigration Reform is to examine immigration trends and effects, to educate the American people on the impacts of sustained high-volume immigration, and to discern, put forward, and advocate immigration policies that will best serve American environmental, societal, and economic interests today and into the future." Among FAIR's goals is to "reduce legal immigration levels from over one million presently to 300,000 a year for a sustained period."[60] This will allow America to manage growth, address environmental concerns and maintain a high quality of life.

FAIR was founded in 1979 by Michigan ophthalmologist John Tanton. He saw the threat from soaring rates of immigration and how the "environment was threatened by overpopulation." He also saw that his liberal colleagues in groups like Planned Parenthood and Sierra Club had no interest in the issue.[61] (No, we don't have to agree with him on everything.)

Something to consider: if you're going to give a "Dreamer" a path to citizenship, are you going to close the gate behind him?

Immigration Is Not a Civil Right

The 1965 immigration reform was presented as the natural outgrowth of the Civil Rights movement, but in fact it had nothing to do with it. Giving equal rights to citizens descended from slaves is completely unrelated to changing which citizens of foreign nations America allows to immigrate here. But it was seen by most as the logical implication.

It was almost an affirmative action program, designed to "rectify" the supposed ethnic imbalances in America. As if any other country seeks perfect "balance" or equal ethnic representation. We're a country, not the Model UN.

Now we have the highest rate of foreign-born people living here since World War I.[62] And that number is still rising. We've imported millions of low-skill immigrants even as we've outsourced or automated most low-skill jobs. We see massive welfare dependency among immigrant families. And our elites, which actively oppose Western Culture as intrinsically racist, discourage these millions of immigrants from assimilating to America.

Welcome to *Blade Runner, 2018.*

CHAPTER THREE

What Is America, Anyway?

We've laid out the political and cultural biases that obscure and distort the policy debate over immigration; the grave practical challenges that the status quo poses America; and the history of immigration's impact on our country. Before we get to solutions, it's time to ask ourselves the one crucial question that too often gets swept under the rug, or lazily half-answered between the lines of opinion-makers' arguments.

Who are we? What does it mean to be an American?

Ask average Americans, and they—surprisingly—agree on some core points. The *Washington Post* analyzed data from the December 2016 View of the Electoral Research (VOTER) Survey, examining "What's very important to being American?"

- 93 percent said "Respecting American institutions and laws"
- 91 percent said "Having American citizenship" (bad news for those who try to tell us illegal immigrants are simply citizens without papers or that it's okay to allow them to vote in American elections)

Did you know?

★ Oppression is not the source of America's success

★ What makes America unique is neither its founding principles nor its ethnic makeup

★ It would be constitutional to require immigrants to renounce Sharia in order to become U.S. citizens

★ America is a Christian nation—in fact, a Protestant one

- 88 percent stressed the importance of accepting people of diverse racial and religious backgrounds (*E pluribus unum* is right on the money)
- 85 percent said speaking English (though that was 96 percent for Republicans, 75 percent for Democrats)[1]

So to summarize, what's very important to being American—according to Americans—is a common passion for the American experiment, a common belief in a color-blind society, and a common language.

Seems like common sense to us.

But what is America itself? What do the Stars and Stripes stand for? What do we see when we hear "The Star-Spangled Banner"? Do we stand up proud or do we kneel? Who exactly do we think we are? If we can't answer that question, our solutions to most problems (especially immigration) will be incoherent, ad hoc, and likely self-defeating.

There are three widely popular views on offer, as we see it. A truthful picture of America would draw on what's accurate in each of these accounts. They are not equally true, of course, but there's at least a smidgen of truth in all three. We'll start with the least persuasive, acknowledging the grains of truth which it contains, and then move on to saner views, ending with a synthesis that accounts for the best of each.

Since none of these theories is completely correct, we'll offer slightly pejorative titles for each: **America the Exploiter, America the Abstraction,** and **America the Happy Accident**.

The unifying theme? Each of these definitions of our country accounts for the relationship between the expansive claims and promises of the Declaration of Independence and the reality of our life as a nation.

America the Exploiter

Leftists who believe in the **America the Exploiter** idea emphasize the gap between theory and practice. They spend most of their study of American history pointing up hypocrisy, broken promises, and imperfect applications of our founding principles. They also read those principles in a completely ahistorical way, through the lens of the radical individualism enshrined in constitutional jurisprudence by Justice Anthony Kennedy in *Planned Parenthood v. Casey* and *Obergefell v. Hodges*. The fact that the Founders would have been appalled at the idea of abortion and same-sex marriage should not be allowed to influence our very contemporary reading of their founding principles. We can just insert our new morality as we go along, with no concern for the original meaning of our nation's founding documents.

For these lefties, immigration restrictions are just part and parcel of the institutionalized racism and elitism that has corrupted America since its founding. In their minds, the Declaration might as well have been written on cloth cut from a Klansman's hood. Still, they can exploit Founding documents like the Declaration (for all its hypocrisy) in their fight for social justice.

Mass immigration from non-Western countries is an essential tool for such leftists in (to quote Barack Obama) "fundamentally transforming" America into a multicultural society where whites must atone for their ancestors' sins by accepting indefinite unequal treatment via affirmative action that disfavors them and anti-discrimination laws that don't protect them. American Exploiters would include Bernie Sanders, Senator Elizabeth Warren, the Reverend Jeremiah Wright, Barack and Michelle Obama, and probably 99 percent of college professors in the humanities and social sciences.

Increasingly, leftists in America hold the view that we have inherited a basically wicked country that became great by displacing the Indians, enslaving Africans, exploiting the working class, and unjustly excluding immigrants. Uncle Sam is a degenerate.

Don't call them "anti-American," though. They don't discriminate. They would say the same of just about any Western country, from Iceland to Ireland. Conversely, they will stick to candy-coated tourist-brochure accounts of any non-Western country, ignoring its moral flaws and airbrushing its (sometimes blood-soaked) history. In fact, the Left will even gang up on ex-Muslims who criticize Sharia, and escapees from Communist countries who point up the cruelties of the Marxist system.

They do this because the Left's very DNA is made not of a double helix, but of double standards. We mean multiculturalism, which dehumanizes people from non-Western cultures by refusing to hold them to the same moral criteria as Westerners. For instance, white Western males can be shunned and shamed for being insufficiently feminist, or refusing to pretend that a castrated man is really a woman. But Arab men get a free pass for throwing gay men off roofs and subjecting their daughters to female genital mutilation. It's as if Western elites had decided to adopt the Third World from a rescue shelter and treat its immigrants forever as exotic, charming, but sometimes mischievous pets.

But virtually every country on earth is the fruit of conquest of past inhabitants, and all but a few are much more oppressive and unequal than America. Most non-Western countries are far worse, except for those that have directly imitated…Anglo-American democracy and capitalism. The "anticolonialism" in which Barack Obama was educated adds Marxist pseudo-analysis to the mix. As Dinesh D'Souza writes, "I believe the most compelling explanation of Obama's actions is that he is, just like his father, an anti-colonialist. Anti-colonialism is the idea that the rich countries got rich by looting the poor countries, and that within the rich countries, plutocratic and corporate elites continue to exploit ordinary citizens."[2] The Reverend Jeremiah Wright, Obama's mentor, pastor, and instructor in Marxist liberation theology, put it more succinctly: "God damn America!"[3] You also can find this "deeply pessimistic vision of the American experience"[4] spelled out in the wildly popular *A People's History of the United States* by political scientist Howard Zinn. FBI files released in 2010 revealed Zinn had not only been a member of Communist Party USA but had lied about it.[5] His bio is a laundry list of radical associations. So naturally, he should be our go-to guy when examining U.S. history. His bestseller contains chapters like "War is the Health of the State," "Slavery Without Submission, Emancipation Without Freedom," and a broadside against the Founders called "Tyranny is Tyranny."

It's bad enough that *A People's History* is fawned over by wealthy celebrity elites like Matt Damon (who featured it in *Good Will Hunting*). But this radical manifesto has now been force-fed to a generation of high school students across our country. It is assigned reading for thousands of college courses. As Georgetown history professor Michael Kazin said, "For Zinn, ordinary Americans seem to live only to fight the rich and haughty and, inevitably, to be fooled by them."[6]

It is no wonder that the American flag makes so many snowflakes scamper to their safe spaces.

Yet *A People's History of the United States*, like the America-the-Exploiter view in general, raises the question: if America is such a roach motel why are so many lining up to check in? The Left's usual answer is to claim that the United States wrecked the countries the newcomers are leaving through capitalism, militarism, or other sins. So we deserve the festering problems caused by unassimilated massive low-skill immigration.

That's apparently Pope Francis's theory. Or so say two leftist journalists who published a recent book laying out his political and economic views, *This Economy Kills: Pope Francis on Capitalism and Social Justice*. As *First Things* noted in a review, "According to Francis, the world is divided into haves and have-nots; the impoverished circumstances and dismal prospects of the latter are principally caused by the former; and the current distribution of power and resources on the international scene is arranged and manipulated by the haves at the expense of the have-nots.... Francis presents himself as a friend of the poor, *and hence* as the great bane and excoriator of their enemies.... He calls for 'revolution,' both cultural or spiritual (#114) and structural. His preferred means is 'dialogue,' but such dialogue is to lead to enormous changes in thinking and living, to the 'radical' reordering of our lives, both individual and communal, at the local, national, and international levels. Francis is a change-agent with comprehensive global designs..."

We don't think Jesus ever said, "Blessed are the poor, for I can use them as a weapon against the rich."

First Things cites "Francis's impassioned calls for western countries to receive refugees and immigrants, regardless of security or other domestic concerns. In his fuller thinking, this sort of open-borders hospitality is not just a Christian obligation and not simply a humanitarian one; it has geopolitical significance and consequences as well. Among other things, these can be seen as *condign punishment* for the north's colonial and capitalist insolence. More than once, the pope has ventured the theologically remarkable thought that natural catastrophes might be Nature's payback for ecological assaults; the same would be true for the contemporary exoduses and migrations that he says occur on a biblical scale today."[7]

What exactly did Germany ever do to Syria to deserve an army of military-age young men strutting its streets, raping women, and demanding Sharia? Belgium might owe reparations to the Congo for its colonialism, but why does it deserve Wahabi Muslims from Turkey and Afghanistan collecting welfare and planning an Islamic state? Let's not even get into all the structural reasons for poverty in Mexico that have absolutely nothing to do with "exploitation" by the Yancqui. (Actually, we will get into those structural reasons in a later chapter.)

It seems that open-borders leftists, even in the Vatican, think in broad strokes and very rough justice.

For those who believe in the bogeyman that is America the Exploiter, mass immigration from non-Western or underdeveloped countries is two things, each equally important:

- A political boon to their favorite electoral causes (immigration has turned California from a Reagan redoubt to Jerry Brown territory—and can do the same for Texas)
- A cultural baptism that will wash away our sins

America the Abstraction

Bizarre as it may seem, neoconservatives who believe in **America the Abstraction** largely agree with that liberal reading of the Founding, except sometimes on abortion. Then they go on to define what is truly American by what coincides with those abstract and ahistorical principles, and seek to marginalize or purge anything that doesn't. They consistently argue that foreign and domestic policy should be guided by those principles alone. This led them—during the George W. Bush administration, and even after—to favor a U.S. foreign policy of promoting democracy first (instead of focusing on U.S. national interests), nation-building in Iraq and Afghanistan, and support for movements like the "Arab Spring." Domestically, it leads them to favor large-scale immigration in the confidence that American principles are so attractive that just learning about them in school and soaking them in on television will make newcomers interchangeable with tenth-generation Americans.

America the Happy Accident

Nationalists view the Declaration more skeptically. They see its principles as partly a rhetorical weapon that our Founders used to gain foreign support for

★ ★ ★
Ugly Americans

Racialists and Alt-Right activists take Nationalist principles to an absurd and immoral extreme, pretending that racial identity was always an essential part of American nationhood. (That was the argument endorsed by the disgraceful *Dred Scott* decision.) In other words, they essentially agree with leftists that the United States was always an exploitative white hegemony based on inequality. They just think that's a good thing, and want to keep it that way.

their attempt to reassert their specifically English liberties. They view the American political system as not an end in itself but a means that a particular, concrete people chose to use to govern itself—the people being primary, not the principles. So they see **America as a Happy Accident** of history. Nationalists worry that the United States is wasting trillions of dollars and degrading its military in the futile attempt to plant democracy and individual rights in nations where neither ever existed—and inadvertently handing power to radical Islamists, who can wield majority power in many Muslim countries (such as Libya). On immigration, Nationalists prefer something closer to America's pre-1965 immigration policy, on the sober assumption that the further someone's culture is from our founding Anglo-American base, the harder it may prove to assimilate him—especially at time when our nation's identity is under unremitting attack by the Left.

We'll propose a synthesis drawing on what is true in the views above and show its implications for immigration policy.

America: The Goose *and* the Golden Egg

In fact what makes America work is a vital tension between two different but equally crucial elements:

1. The Golden Egg: moral, civic, and economic *principles* that could, in theory, be applied to any country on earth, and to any group of immigrants we admitted to America, however large. These principles are simply true for every human being, and we must insist on that fact. In contrast to the Left's relativism and politics of group resentment, these principles offer an inclusive, persuasive program which should appeal to any voter of good will. Key among those principles are truths such as "All men are created equal," "Every human being has equal value and dignity," and "Judeo-Christian religious faith guards our freedom." If pursued consistently, these principles should always produce a more peaceful, prosperous, free country than would otherwise be possible.

2. The Goose: real, existing, historically-founded *facts* that explain why these principles have worked here in America while failing spectacularly when tried elsewhere—for instance in the Latin American republics that declared independence shortly after the thirteen colonies did, wrote similar declarations and comparable constitutions, and promptly degenerated into a two-hundred-year cycle of dictatorships and chaos. The most important of these facts was the dominance of a tolerant, Anglo-Protestant culture grounded in some eight hundred years of English resistance to oppressive governments. Change this fact too radically or too quickly, and the principles we treasure will wither and die. Another critical fact is broad economic and social mobility, which has generally made Americans unwilling to tax the successful to death because they hope someday to join them—or to watch their children do so. Income inequality in America is both greater than in Europe and much less politically explosive than there.

★ ★ ★

The Fable of the Goose & the Golden Egg

There was once a Countryman who possessed the most wonderful Goose you can imagine, for every day when he visited the nest, the Goose had laid a beautiful, glittering, golden egg.

The Countryman took the eggs to market and soon began to get rich. But it was not long before he grew impatient with the Goose because she gave him only a single golden egg a day. He was not getting rich fast enough.

Then one day, after he had finished counting his money, the idea came to him that he could get all the golden eggs at once by killing the Goose and cutting it open. But when the deed was done, not a single golden egg did he find, and his precious Goose was dead.

Those who have plenty want more and so lose all they have.[8]

85

The word "establishment" in reference to the GOP's donors, thinkers, and leaders has been bandied about almost to the point of meaninglessness. But we can reclaim some use for it in light of the Egg and the Goose—and explain the profound alienation that was exposed by the 2016 election. Those who supported Donald Trump in the 2016 election thought that the GOP establishment had mastered the art of shining and selling the Golden Egg, but forgot to care for the Goose.

By promoting massive low-skill immigration from countries (ranging from Mexico to Syria) that are completely devoid of America's formative Anglo-Protestant ethos, and into a spendthrift American welfare state, GOP elites have served the interests of large companies seeking cheap labor. But they have endangered the crucial social matrix that makes the free market and a free society possible—a matrix that the great free market economist and anti-Nazi hero Wilhelm Röpke warned is the very foundation of freedom. At the same time, these politicians have typically urged or led the United States into costly, futile, or counter-productive attempts to sow or even build "democracy" in parts of the world where it has never existed. And may never exist. Critics describe the philosophy of George W. Bush, Jeb Bush, John McCain, Lindsey Graham, and Paul Ryan as reducible to this bumper sticker: "Invade the World, Invite the World."

Conversely, the neocons and other GOP establishment figures point with grave concern to the rise of angry, racially motivated white activists. Some of the Alt-Right reject America's founding principles altogether. Some even denounce the Constitution itself as an antiquated "piece of paper" that stands in the way of their pursuing what they consider the legitimate self-interests of the "white community." Indeed, these activists accept many of the multiculturalist principles of the Left and seek to hijack them for the benefit of a new political movement: a white ethnic lobby, with race-specific demands that take no account of American liberty or universal moral principles. This tribal cult scrambles the Golden Egg, but kneels to worship the Goose.

The eruption of such a movement is a pathological phenomenon, but it is a symptom as much as a sickness. It's the noise the Goose makes as it's dying. Take the reckless, cynical willingness of leftist elites to trash Western culture, vilify our national heritage, and treat tolerant Christianity as something worse than jihadist Islam—then add to that the total lack of interest that conservative elites have shown in the care and feeding, the defense and preservation of any aspect of that culture beyond "small government" and the "free market," and it's no surprise that white identity politics emerged as an ugly reaction.

Back in 2003, when Golden Egg enthusiasts had almost completely captured the think tanks, magazines, and other institutions of conservatism, John Zmirak wrote a long "think piece" titled "America the Abstraction" warning against the dangers of unmoored ideology. Its message is still relevant today:

> If you are trying to boil down citizenship to its philosophically respectable components, and if ideology is all you are interested in, then it does not really matter where you were born. Or who your parents were. Or whom you love. Or the hymns you know by heart, the folk tales you treasure, the God you worship. None of these merely human matters measures up, ideologically speaking. None of them can be enshrined in a manifesto, or beamed across the world via Voice of America, or exported in music videos. They do not raise the GDP, or lower the interest rate, or increase our command of oil reserves. They cannot be harnessed to drive the engine of globalization. Therefore, to some people, these things do not matter. Such pieties can be harnessed in the run-up to a war, can form part of the Army recruitment ads and propaganda campaigns, and may even find their way into presidential speeches. But essentially there is no difference between

a fourth-generation American and an Afghan refugee who just landed at JFK—so long as they both accept the same ideology.

How did we get to this pass? How did conservatism, which once centered on the fierce defense of tradition, religion, and particularism, turn into an ideology—that is, a philosophy in arms, a political system shorn of its ties to real people and places, slimmed down by dropping historical baggage, packaged for export on the global market of ideas?

The piece went on to explain how the Cold War had inspired the conservative movement to create a kind of Americanism that would compete with Marxism as an ideology on the international stage. Thus, "Increasingly, America was defined according to the most expansive, abstract reading of the Declaration of Independence, combined with a version of market economics well-suited to the unrestricted 'pursuit of happiness.'" But that's a very incomplete definition.[9]

In 2017, Rich Lowry and Ramesh Ponnuru of *National Review* argued, along the same lines, for a "benign nationalism" that would take more account of the Goose side of the equation:

> The outlines of a benign nationalism are not hard to discern. It includes loyalty to one's country: a sense of belonging, allegiance, and gratitude to it. And this sense attaches to the country's people and culture, not just to its political institutions and laws. Such nationalism includes solidarity with one's countrymen, whose welfare comes before, albeit not to the complete exclusion of, that of foreigners. When this nationalism finds political expression, it supports a federal government that is jealous of its sovereignty, forthright and unapologetic about advancing its people's interests, and mindful of the need for national cohesion.[10]

Jonah Goldberg, in the same magazine, respectfully differed, declaring his preference for the Golden Egg:

> Our shrines are to patriots who upheld very specific American ideals. Our statues of soldiers commemorate heroes who died for something very different from what other warriors have fought and died for millennia. Every one of them—immigrants included—took an oath to defend not just some soil but our Constitution and by extension the ideals of the Founding. Walk around any European hamlet or capital and you will find statues of men who fell in battle to protect their tribe from another tribe. That doesn't necessarily diminish the nobility of their deaths or the glory of their valor, but it is quite simply a very different thing they were fighting for....[11]

Ben Shapiro also joined the debate on the Golden Egg side:

> Conservatives love America because we believe it is a nation founded on an idea. Our interests ought to prevail because our principles ought to prevail: limited government, individual liberty, God-given natural rights, localism in politics, religious freedom, freedom of speech and of the press, and so forth. If America ceased to believe those things or stand for them, we would not deserve to win. "Make America Great Again" would then ring hollow with the same blood-and-soil nationalistic violence of the Old World. If greatness is measured in utilitarian terms rather than ideological ones, nationalism is merely tribalism broadened, a way of valuing the collective over the individual.[12]

Of course, the critics of nationalism are right, up to a point. They correctly warn that an unreflective attachment to hearth and home, totem and tribe can erupt in the kind of ugliness we see around the world, which took its most infamous form in Hitler's Germany.

But that's not the only kind of danger. Countries bound together only by an abstract ideology can be very dangerous too—as we see not just from the Soviet Union and revolutionary France, but more recently in the empire created by ISIS and the relentless drive for power of the Muslim Brotherhood.

Goldberg and Shapiro recognize this, of course. They read their history, and know that ideologies can be dangerous. *They just don't seem to think that America's can be.* They don't recognize that American principles, while truer than most, can also be abused and applied to evil ends.

But isn't that exactly what happened when our judicial elites declared that our Constitution enshrined the right to abortion? That liberty means we get to redefine reality to suit our desires and our convenience? That human dignity requires same-sex marriage?

We might rightly say that these are false inferences from our principles, but this is currently the official governing philosophy of the United States legal system. Stripped by judicial intellectuals of their tolerant, Protestant Christian context (the "originalist" reading of the Constitution that Justice Scalia insisted on), our founding principles can prove very dangerous indeed; they have been fatal to almost sixty million unborn American children.

Our Founders were fallen men, and their ideas were not divinely revealed from heaven. The profound truths that did emerge in America's founding were not some brilliant ideas that Enlightenment thinkers came up with out of the blue. They had emerged over centuries in a very specific context: the Christian soil of England, with its Saxon resistance to political authority and its Protestant obsession with spiritual independence. That was the soil the Tree of Liberty grew in. Scrape it away, replace it with alien sand or secular gravel, and it might wither. Or to go back to our first metaphor, the Goose might keel over and die.

The Poison of White Nationalism

There's a French proverb: "To understand all is to forgive all." The sentiment rolls off the tongue. It makes you sound wise, compassionate, and cosmopolitan. It even seems, if not quite Christian, at any rate *Christian-ish*. We can't call the idea orthodox, since God *does* understand all. But He only forgives the penitent. He comprehends Satan perfectly, but that's not going to open any doors Upstairs.

We can understand Satan too, if only a little. Every time we choose our own will over God's, we repeat his "*non serviam.*" When we indulge in envy we get really close to the hot, beating heart of Hell. Milton managed extraordinary sympathy for the devil in *Paradise Lost*. There he pictured the fallen angel, still picking the scabs where his pride had seared off his glory, skulking in Eden. Watching the two naked innocents. Hating them for their happiness, and planning to take it away.

It's in this sense that we can understand why some white Americans are tempted by white identity politics. White people are fallen like everyone else. They too are subject to tribalist sympathies—just as black, Hispanic, and Asian people are. What's more, the Left has gone so far in demonizing whiteness, maleness, Christian faith, and sane, middle class life, that it's easy to overreact. It's diabolically tempting.

But no one is going to forgive you for dabbling in white identity politics. That might not sound fair. (*But MOM! Al Sharpton's mom lets him do it!*) Earthly life isn't fair. It *really* wasn't fair for black people enslaved for two hundred years and denied civil rights for another one hundred. We live in a fallen world, and it's our task to make the best of it. Not to whine, act out, and make things even worse.

> ## America's Principles Gone Astray
>
> "At the heart of liberty is the right to define one's own concept of existence, of meaning, of the universe, and of the mystery of human life.... people have organized intimate relationships and made choices that define their views of themselves and their places in society, in reliance on the availability of abortion...."
>
> —Justice Anthony Kennedy, *Planned Parenthood v. Casey*

91

★ ★ ★

Brothers beneath the Skin

If Al Sharpton, Louis Farrakhan, David Duke, and Richard Spencer all agree on a course of action, don't you think it's a safe bet to do the opposite?

Inspired in large part by appeals to gospel justice, our national civic religion changed, for the better, during the Civil Rights Movement. We were deeply and rightly ashamed at the sight of armed cops beating up passive, peaceful demonstrators, turning vicious dogs loose on them—of churches smoking in ruins with the corpses of little black girls bombed by masked Klan cowards.

And good people don't want to go back.

We do want to get our nation's borders under control. We do want to stop crime and keep cops safe on the job. And we want to fix the welfare system, so it doesn't create another generation of hopeless dependents. None of those goals rests on racial animus. They are good things that wise people of every ethnicity can get behind.

Conservative black economists Thomas Sowell and Walter Williams favor all those things, while white leftists like Tim Kaine and Hillary Clinton oppose them.

If you tell people that the way to resist multiculturalism and out-of-control immigration is the white tribalism of the Klan, of Margaret Sanger, even of Adolf Hitler, you know what's going to happen? The Left will win. On every front. For the rest of our lives, and our children's lives too. The white nationalists will accomplish just as much as the Black Panthers did when they led riots that burned down their own neighborhoods. The white racialists would turn America into a vast, white Watts or Newark. Why should we let them? It will only hurt everyone except the class of race-hustlers who make a living by stoking division.

Yes, it is true that a strain of tribalism goes back to the American colonists, who following fallen human nature, hunted and displaced Indians and thought nothing of buying black slaves. But let's not pretend there's anything uniquely white or American about that.

The Han Chinese ran China. The Arabs ran Arabia, and overran most of the Mediterranean. When the Goths conquered Rome, they didn't ask themselves whether they were exercising "Goth privilege." (Would that mean having first access to jet black hair dye and emo music?) The Poles want to dominate Poland—especially after centuries of other people marching in and ruining the place.

But America is something better, rarer, more fragile than a traditional ethno-state, held together by a kin-based nationalism.

As the great conservative thinker Samuel Huntington observed, what unites us, white and black, is our shared culture: tolerant Anglo-Protestantism.

America wasn't formed mainly by the Enlightenment principles of the Declaration of Independence. Because, as we have already seen, virtually every Latin American colony that broke off from Spain, from Mexico to Venezuela, embraced similar principles. But ordered liberty didn't take root in those lands, for deep cultural reasons.

Thomas Jefferson's words were not some global panacea. They were just a way of universalizing and making palatable to the French (who paid for our Revolution) *traditional English liberties*.

Those liberties grew from Christian faith and Saxon hatred of tyranny. They were always implicitly for everyone, and they now bless people from India to Hong Kong, from Belfast to the Falkland Islands. But the English were the pioneers of ordered liberty. They were the

★ ★ ★
When in Rome
Even American Catholics have Protestant political habits, as Italian Jews have Catholic ones.

first nation in history to emancipate their slaves—then go to war against the slave trade. A British judge ruled that according to Common Law, British air was free—so that any slave who breathed it was thereby emancipated.

That's our heritage, and it belongs to every last one of us. We won't trade it for some sick, squalid cult of DNA-based group narcissism. Yes, we understand the temptation to vicious, self-destructive and unpatriotic tribalism. We just renounce it, along with Satan, all his works, and all his pomps.

Paul Ryan: Polishing the Egg, Cooking the Goose

For more than a decade, current GOP House Speaker Paul Ryan has worked with far-left Democrat Representative Luis V. Gutiérrez to promote immigration amnesty and resist real border security measures. Ryan's advocacy even won him the Democrat's endorsement as Speaker in 2015. As Gutiérrez wrote:

> I have worked closely with Paul Ryan for years on the immigration issue and I know he supports sensible, bipartisan reform, just like most Americans and most Members of the House....
>
> As a person of faith, a person of conscience, and a person who deeply believes in American exceptionalism, Paul Ryan supports legal immigration and getting immigrants already here into the system so we can improve enforcement and secure the rights of working people and employers. I do not doubt that Ryan supports sensible immigration reform, but some in the GOP will try to disqualify anyone who supports what the majority of Americans support.
>
> In a nutshell, this inability to support legal immigration and legality for immigrants is at the heart of the Republican Party's national problem and why they will be shut out of the White House for the foreseeable future. The coalition of women, African-Americans, Asians, gays and lesbians, environmentalists, young

people and Latinos that the Republican Party rejects has formed an ironclad majority that will keep them out of the presidency.[13]

Almost exactly twelve months later, Donald Trump was elected president. Not with any meaningful support by Paul Ryan, however. Even as Muslim mass immigration into Europe was enabling a series of terrorist attacks unprecedented since the 1930s and ISIS was trying to weaponize Muslim immigrants for terrorist strikes in America, Ryan was condemning Trump's talk of reducing the influx of Muslims into the United States. As the AP reported during the 2015 presidential primary race,

> Speaker Paul Ryan on Tuesday criticized Republican presidential candidate Donald Trump's proposal to bar Muslims from entering the U.S., saying such views are "not what this party stands for and more importantly it's not what this country stands for."
>
> Speaking to reporters after a closed-door GOP caucus meeting, Ryan addressed Trump's remarks without mentioning him by name. The speaker said he doesn't normally comment on the presidential race but was making an exception.
>
> "Freedom of religion is a fundamental constitutional principle," Ryan said. "This is not conservatism. What was proposed yesterday is not what this party stands for. And more importantly, it's not what this country stands for."[14]

The First Amendment, curiously, does not protect foreign citizens living abroad. Constitutional scholars and Supreme Court decisions have consistently agreed that the United States has an absolute sovereign right to accept or reject foreign nationals on any basis whatsoever. Okay, so it may not be unconstitutional to limit Muslim migrants. But surely it's immoral, even un-American, right?

Wrong. Here's why.

The Problem with Islam

Imagine if the bigoted Westboro Baptist Church took over the Southern Baptist Convention and Pope Francis were replaced with the renegade bishop Richard Williamson, who questions the Holocaust. Then swap out the vast majority of Catholic bishops for various Holocaust deniers. Imagine further that for all of its history Christianity had been committed to enforcing in law the harshest punishments mentioned in the Old Testament—including the death penalty for astrologers, adulterers, and disobedient children.

Now pretend that virtually all Christian Churches—Catholic, Protestant, and Orthodox—agreed that religious coercion was an intrinsic part of Christianity, which ought to dominate the entire planet, by force if necessary, subjugating members of every other religion where possible, especially Jews. Imagine further that Christians today regarded Jews as despicable renegades who had falsified their own scriptures in order to hijack divine revelation. Imagine that every Christian was told by the gospel itself to wage a "crusade" against unbelievers (armed and unarmed), in imitation of Christ.

Imagine that Christian immigrants formed in the churches that they built in their new countries political cells dedicated to promoting an aggressively militant Global Christendom, with lavish funding from the Vatican. While many Christians remained rather lukewarm and lax, a lively minority in every country that had a Christian presence actively identified as "crusaders." Christian families were urged by their clergy to keep up a higher birth rate than their neighbors—if need be by relying on generous public welfare programs—so that they could someday impose Christian supremacy in the new societies where they were living.

Christians in poor countries would be encouraged by their clergy to emigrate to rich non-Christian countries in order to wage the "Crusade of the Cradle." Periodically, Christians would be arrested for defying secular law—for stoning a disobedient child or adulteress, say—and Christians would respond by claiming that they are subject only to Church law. Oh yes, and picture just one more thing: that 99.5 percent of the murderous suicide attacks in the world in 2015 had been committed by Christianists engaged in "the crusade."[15]

In this fantasy world, imagine that a non-Christian society such as Japan were inundated with would-be Christian immigrants clamoring to join a fast-growing minority of Christians already present—in the context of recurring high-profile terrorist attacks on Japanese citizens by violent Christian crusaders. Would Japanese politicians who opposed such a Christian influx be bigots? Should they be accused of reverting to fascism, or wishing to reenact the Rape of Nanking, simply because they did not wish to open their nation's doors to people whose deepest-held beliefs were intrinsically violent, aggressive, and focused on dominating their neighbors?

Would citizens who listened to those politicians themselves be bigots? Would Japan be betraying its post-war, post-fascist democratic constitution if it chose to accept other immigrants instead? Absolutely not. It would be doing the first, most basic duty of any government: protecting its citizens and their basic human rights against the aggression of outsiders.

Neither would America be betraying its tolerant culture by rejecting Muslim immigrants today. Yes, there are many kind and decent Muslims. But every orthodox Muslim holds that Sharia should be the law of the land in every country in the world and that Muslim men are duty-bound to engage in jihad until this is the case. Every orthodox Muslim believes that the proper penalty for adultery, or homosexuality, or leaving Islam, is death. Every orthodox Muslim believes that polygamy is acceptable and that girls can be married as young as nine—since that was the age of Muhammad's youngest wife, and everything Muhammad did in his life is morally good and worthy of imitation.

These are the facts, stubborn and ugly as sin and death. We don't want to believe this about Islam precisely because the facts are unpleasant. Much easier, isn't it, to pretend that the media are telling the truth about Islam, that it is a "religion of peace" inexplicably hijacked and perverted for evil purposes—over and over and over again, by its own highest clergy, seminaries, universities, and governments that speak in its name?

The stark truth is that the more orthodox a Muslim is, the less he fits into Western society, or into any society committed to ordered liberty.

Islam, which includes Sharia as the Bible includes miracles, is completely incompatible with American freedom and public order—as incompatible as Soviet Communism, which for decades led U.S. authorities (via the McCarran Act) to ban members of Communist parties from immigrating to America.[16] Because of our Constitution we must protect the religious freedom of every citizen. So the United States never deported or persecuted native-born Communists, and it shouldn't trample the rights of native-born or naturalized Muslim citizens. But the presence of devoted Communists was a challenge to America, and during the Cold War it presented a security threat.

The same is true for devout Muslims in America today—who if they are citizens, have every right to preach Islam and urge their fellow citizens to adopt Islamic law. Precisely because our Constitution offers such a broad protection of religious freedom, we must minimize the number of orthodox Muslims who come here each year to enjoy it. The optimum number going forward would be zero.

These facts have nothing to do with race, in case we must make that explicit. Islam, like Communism, is race-neutral, since it wishes to rule all the world. The United States should welcome with open arms the thousands of Arab Christians, Yezidis, and Asian or African ex-Muslims who flee Sharia tyranny, and it should reject blue-eyed, blonde-haired orthodox Muslims.

We should first focus, as President Trump did in his 2017 executive orders, on simply cutting immigration quotas from countries with active Islamist movements. But if that proves ineffective, there is simply no substitute for imposing, by law, a ban on immigration to America by those who believe in Sharia—which is a core element of Islam. The questions on the applications for citizenship and residency would need to be explicit, asking the applicant to renounce "any religion or religious law that limits the freedom of Americans to change religion, preach freely, for or blaspheme against any faith whatsoever."

Yes, some Muslims would lie—especially since their faith itself makes room for deceiving unbelievers in service of Islam.[17] But because their admission to the United States was conditional on this affirmation, immigrants who later engaged in jihadist propaganda could be deported—as the United States deported Nazis who slipped into the United States after World War II by lying about their records.

Americans aren't doing ourselves any favors by pretending that our Muslim neighbors are really Mennonites. As citizens with a solemn moral duty to pass along an America as free and as safe as the one we were blessed to inherit, we have no right to comfort ourselves with happy fables, to lubricate our progress by betraying our core principles, to collude in the self-censorship that is blacking out the news of real threats. If we do, we will end up with neither our birthright, nor even a mess of pottage.

Paul Ryan won't get his Golden Eggs, just the limp form of a dead Goose.

Compare and Contrast: The United States versus Mexico

Mexico is a vast, complex, and beautiful country full of hard-working people of enormous creativity and faith, which has for most of its history been crassly misgoverned—wasting its great potential, and driving millions to flee their homes for America, in defiance of our just and democratically enacted immigration laws.

The stark contrast between American and Mexican history can be traced all the way back to the culture and politics of the nations that colonized them. The English who settled in North America came from a kingdom where the Magna Carta had prevailed for more than centuries, guaranteeing due process and property rights. The rule of the king of England was dependent on the consent of Parliament. Local government was strong, and much of the power decentralized. The English Reformation, for all the cruelty that was practiced on both sides, had underlined the need for restraints on royal power, as non-conforming Protestants cited medieval Catholic precedents in Common Law to protect their political and religious freedom.

By contrast, the kingdom of Spain had made itself religiously homogeneous in 1492 when it expelled the last Jews and Muslims. In 1520–1521 the Spanish Crown crushed the revolts of localists. Its kings repealed the *fueros*, the Spanish Magna Cartas that had once guaranteed the rights of citizens and small communities. Spain's kings rejected as inefficient and antiquated medieval restraints on monarchs and governed according to the new theory of absolute monarchy. Order was not seen as something that grew organically from the ground, but as a magnetic force that proceeded from a single all-powerful center.

These contrasting political philosophies set the tone for the histories of two nations. While English colonies developed vibrant town councils and colonial legislatures, mostly rejecting attempts to impose royal governors from England, the provinces of New Spain were run by appointees arriving from Spain. The initiative for laws came not from the citizens of Mexico City or Monterrey, but from faraway Madrid.

Nor did the Spanish legal system provide the same robust protections for property rights as those English citizens and colonists could rely on.

When England tried to impose protectionism on the residents of its colonies, their local governments resisted, winking at smuggling to avoid the crippling tariffs. By contrast, New Spain's governors were perfectly willing to govern that province in Spain's (not New Spain's) interests, suppressing whole industries if Spain found the competition obnoxious. The path to wealth in New Spain lay through royal patronage and vast land grants, not industry or commerce.

When the United States and Mexico cast off their colonial masters, each followed in the tracks which their past had lain down. While the American Founders built elaborate checks and balances into their Constitution and reserved most taxing and governing power to states and even towns, the elites who seized power in newly founded Mexico continued to act like Spanish grandees, seeing those whom they governed not so much as citizens but as subjects.

It was only the Catholic Church that preserved some land for Indians— and ambitious descendants of the conquistadors would gradually steal it in the name of "freeing" Mexico from the dominance of the Church. The periodic revolutions and coups d'état that marked the transitions of power in Mexico were not philosophically driven movements like the American Revolution, but mostly the acts of strongmen like General Santa Anna who sought unaccountable power. Sometimes they used that power, as in the 1920s, to persecute clergy and churchgoers—trying to

A Book You're Not Supposed to Read

The Mystery of Capital: Why Capitalism Triumphs in the West and Fails Everywhere Else by Peruvian economist Hernando de Soto (Basic Books, 2000) demonstrates how crucial property rights are to raising people from poverty.

break the back of the only institution that could resist the centralized state. The faithful priests and peasants who took up arms in resistance (the Cristeros) nearly toppled that evil government.

Through all these historical traumas, the hard-working and long-suffering people of Mexico have forged a powerful sense of their own nationhood, which ideologues sometimes have fanned into intolerant nationalism. The socialist Party of Institutionalized Revolution rode such sentiments to power and in 1938 seized the property of the (foreign-built) oil industry and turned it into a crony capitalist monopoly. Such economic populism, whether practiced in Mexico or Venezuela, has a predictable effect: it starves local industries of much-needed investment and helps make a few fat cats rich, while impoverishing the majority.

For all of that, the United States is the aggrieved party in the immigration crisis. While our neighbors in Mexico deserve our goodwill, respect, and prayers, their country is rife with social problems that we should not be importing in the form of millions of low-skill migrants whose political and social expectations have been formed by crony socialism. That's how you turn Texas into California, and nobody wants that—apart from unelectable Democrats in the Lone Star State.

A Sane Synthesis: Samuel Huntington

So we ought to treasure both the Golden Egg that is ordered liberty and the hale old Goose that produces it. We also need to avoid fragmentation mines like white nationalism, multiculturalism, and abstract Americanism. Happily, a saner view is out there. In fact, it's the sane, prudent view that governed American immigration policy for most of our history—right up through 1965. That view is neither racist, xenophobic, nor intolerant. But it does look out for the real historical particularity of America, and protects our civic heritage. The best spokesman for it was the late Samuel Huntington.

His last book is erudite and readable, analytical but urgent, a work of political science which the author admits he wrote as "a patriot."

That is, he wrote it from a conscious, explicit desire to preserve and defend America. Not just its political institutions, or the explicit ideology which undergirds them, but also the concrete, shared reality that is America. Much of that, Huntington demonstrates, is the result not of inexorable historical progress or the unfolding of mankind's deepest yearnings and some obscure divine decree, but of happy historical accidents.

Among these accidents, the author is not embarrassed to point out, is the national character which marked the North American colonists. He means their "Anglo-Protestant culture." Huntington points out that literally dozens of other nations were founded at almost the same time by Enlightened liberal Freemasons from Colombia to Paraguay, yet few of them persevered in their liberal institutions. Why did Bolivar's Republic founder into chaos and tyranny while Washington's prospered and stayed free? Because political seeds can only flourish when they fall in fertile ground.

The soil in which liberal, decentralized government could survive—insofar as it has survived—was one that had been prepared for centuries before Jefferson ever set pen to paper. Huntington points to the suspicion of centralized authority which persisted in the dominant (Presbyterian, Quaker, and Puritan) strands of Protestantism to which the overwhelming majority of American settlers adhered. Then to the century or more of congregational (rather than papal or episcopal) decision-making through which these churches were governed. And finally to the very worldly work ethic that characterized men of these creeds.

These churches, he says, were the "reformation of the Reformation." He contrasts their anti-authoritarianism, pragmatism, and general

A Book You're Not Supposed to Read

Who Are We? The Challenges to America's National Identity by Samuel P. Huntington (Simon & Schuster, 2004).

suspicion of institutions with the ways of Anglicans and Catholics—whose faith entails deference to established authority, resignation in the face of suffering, and a pious reverence for poverty. Indeed, these are stereotypes, but who can look at Mexico and Texas (for instance) and fail to see their basis in fact?

This Anglo-Protestant root was planted by America's earliest settlers—whom Huntington carefully distinguishes from immigrants. The Puritans of Massachusetts, the Quakers of Pennsylvania, and the Scots-Irish of Tennessee were not impoverished individuals asking admittance of a developed, preexisting polity to which they were willing to assimilate. They were alien invaders, arriving in groups with clearly defined communal beliefs, determined to buy or wrest a continent away from divided, mutually hostile tribes of hunter-gatherers. That is not the situation faced by contemporary immigrants to the United States—at least, not yet.

With loving detail, Huntington shows how members of every ethnic group that arrived in the United States came to accept the cultural and political mores of its Anglo-Protestant Founders. Jews who had not been not particularly observant in the Old Country established synagogues so they could attend weekly services like the Protestants. Catholics embraced the separation of Church and State—eventually dragging their mother Church after them. Even when religious groups set up their own parochial schools to resist the steady pressure of Protestantization imposed in the public ones, they invariably laid heavy emphasis on patriotism, mastery of English, and the virtues of "Americanism." Such institutions of Americanization, Huntington warns, have largely broken down—leaving degraded commercial culture and mass media as the sole means by which new Americans learn the ways of their adopted country.

Huntington analyzes other developed and developing countries, in comparison with America, to suggest four different kinds of national identity:

1. Ethnic—based on perceptions of a close-knit ethnic group. See Japan, Germany, Ireland, and the early American colonies.
2. Racial—based on visible differences among peoples. Such a unifying principle, Huntington argues, inspired white Americans of various ethnicities once they had begun to intermarry and assimilate—until we realized that it is morally repugnant during the Civil Rights Movement.
3. Cultural—based on shared ways of living, unspoken preconceptions, and social mores. This mode of identification, Huntington suggests, is what unites most Americans today. But it can be undermined by the racialism implicit in identity politics and affirmative action, and by the mass immigration of people from a single nation with a compelling alternative culture, such as Mexico. Huntington warned, presciently, that these abuses of our system might well reawaken an intolerant white nationalism.
4. Propositional, based on ideological maxims derived from political theory. Nations defined this way included Jacobin France and the Soviet Union. This principle of organization—surely the most fragile—is the only one accepted as morally viable by both liberal and neoconservative theorists today, from Barack Obama on the Left to Paul Ryan and John Kasich on the center-right.

Huntington concludes that the United States simply cannot be described honestly as anything but a Christian nation. Its particular mode of Christianity, however, is *intrinsically* tolerant, individualistic, even entrepreneurial. He cites Irving Kristol's famous advice to American Jews: accept and welcome the country's Christian orientation, which has guaranteed for them an environment almost entirely free of the deadly bigotry they encountered in other societies.

Furthermore, Huntington argues, most of the advances that America has seen towards equal opportunity and social reform have been driven by gospel values—in fact, by explicitly Christian movements from abolitionism to the Civil Rights Movement, rather than by socialist activism, as happened through much of Europe. It is in this core of Christian values—which now encompasses Catholics, welcomes Jews, and accepts other more alien faiths so long as they accept the fundamental principle of tolerant co-existence—that Huntington hopes to ground the unified American identity of the future.

Huntington has it exactly right. What's great about America grew from real, particular, fragile roots in historical accidents. What history built, policy can wreck. The America that accepted millions of immigrants and gave them a path from poverty, that embraced the Civil Rights movement and welcomed the world, needs to take a break to figure out how to get itself together again. We treasure the Golden Eggs, but it's time to offer some heat, shelter, and food to the poor abused Goose.

CHAPTER FOUR

Who Backs Our Unsustainable Status Quo?

In chapter one we laid out the mess our immigration system is in and the chaos that mass immigration, illegal and legal, sows in our country. In chapter two we charted the course from Alexander Hamilton's "harmony of Ingredients" to Ted Kennedy's army of chain immigrants. From assimilation to identity politics. From *E pluribus unum* to *Adios, American Dream*. Chapter three outlined the conflicting theories of what America is, and how the misconceived ones (on the Left and establishment Right) help block every sane attempt to control our borders.

Given the financial, human, and societal costs that are tearing up our social fabric, surely every American must be on board with fixing our immigration problem. It's like choosing chocolate cake over cow pies at a birthday party, right?

Wrong. Some people are just fine with the stench. Let's see exactly who.

Cui Bono?

And let's ask why. One relevant question to ask about opposition to real immigration reform is *Cui bono?* No, that's not a question about the lead

Did you know?

★ Sixty-two percent of naturalized immigrants favor the Democrats; 25 percent, the Republicans

★ Latino icon and union organizer Cesar Chavez was a fervent supporter of deporting illegal aliens

★ The purchasing power of the American worker peaked four decades ago

★ Twenty percent of all cooks in American restaurants—and a third of dishwashers—are illegal immigrants

singer for U2, though his taste in eyeglasses ought to raise a question or two. It's the Latin phrase meaning "Who benefits?" Of course we can't completely discredit a person's political view just because it entails his self-interest. Otherwise we'd dismiss the concerns of any taxpayer who favored lower tax rates. But what about when the self-interest involved is illegitimate? When it's something sleazy—when an undeserved benefit is going unacknowledged while the activist pretends that he's only weighing in for high-minded reasons? There's a shockingly long list of such hypocritical and selfish reasons why some favor our current immigration chaos or even wish to make matters worse. Let's look at some of the Cuis and how they Bono.

The Democratic Party: Counterfeiting Votes

Once the party of America's working class, the Democrats seem to have abandoned even the effort to win back blue-collar voters, and given up on loyalty to the America that really exists. As their academic allies tell them constantly, America as founded is hopelessly wicked. What value America has can be found by taking a few of our Founding principles and teasing them out of context to outrageously broad conclusions that would have horrified not just Washington and Madison but John F. Kennedy, Hubert Humphrey, and even George McGovern.

Perhaps the turning point was the Obama presidency, which gave us eight long years of globalist, anti-colonialist sermons by a president who apparently wanted to turn the United States into just another member state of the European Union. It became clear that our internationalist president who grew up abroad attending Muslim schools wasn't the only American to feel more like a citizen of the world than a citizen of the United States. Looking out for American poor people and working class schmoes seemed suddenly so…parochial. Or worse. The Democrats have taken to suggesting that being more concerned about the problems of our fellow Americans than about those of foreigners is somehow racist. They've worked their way into a tight corner on this issue, as some worried pundits have noticed.

But the party's leaders aren't concerned. They look at the huddled masses across the Rio Grande or in the Customs section of JFK Airport and they see…votes.

Byron York has reported, "A 2012 study of 2,900 foreign-born, naturalized immigrants… showed that about 62 percent identified themselves as Democrats, while 25 percent identified as Republicans, and 13 percent identified as independents."[1]

Immigrants provide Democrats easy reliable votes in their effort to expand government. In 2014 the Center for Immigration Studies published a study digging into the numbers. Researcher James Gimpel of the University of Maryland found that

★ ★ ★

Undivided Loyalties

Democratic Representative Luis Gutiérrez of Illinois has been called "the most passionate, tireless, and nettlesome voice in Congress on immigration matters." He makes no bones about who he works for, telling *Newsweek*, "I have only one loyalty and that's to the immigrant community."[2] We believe him. Whether that "one loyalty" is compatible with the oath of office he has taken to "support and defend the Constitution of the United States against all enemies, foreign and domestic" is another question.

- Immigrants, particularly Hispanics and Asians, have policy preferences when it comes to the size and scope of government that are more closely aligned with progressives than with conservatives. As a result, survey data show a two-to-one party identification with Democrats over Republicans.
- By increasing income inequality and adding to the low-income population (e.g. immigrants and their minor children account for one-fourth of those in poverty and one-third of the uninsured) immigration likely makes all voters more supportive

of redistributive policies championed by Democrats to support disadvantaged populations.

- There is evidence that immigration may cause more Republican-oriented voters to move away from areas of high immigrant settlement leaving behind a more lopsided Democrat majority.[3]

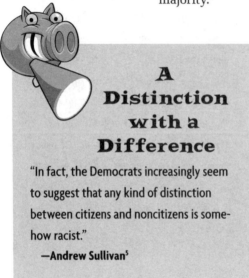

A Distinction with a Difference

"In fact, the Democrats increasingly seem to suggest that any kind of distinction between citizens and noncitizens is somehow racist."

—Andrew Sullivan[5]

In some cities, Democrats are even pushing to allow illegal immigrants to vote. In 2017, a majority of the city council in College Park, Maryland, approved a measure to allow just that. Thankfully, they needed more than a simple majority to make the measure stick.[4]

More commonly, Democrats are a little more discreet, and simply make it de facto easy for non-citizens to vote by fighting every reasonable effort at voter ID laws, which they equate with the Jim Crow measures that kept freed slaves away from the polls. The Democrats take a condescending attitude toward black and Hispanic American citizens— as if they were shiftless hobos with no capacity to prove their identities.

Democratic support for illegal immigration surprises even liberal writer Peter Beinhart. He wrote in the *Atlantic* in 2017, "In 2008, the Democratic platform called undocumented immigrants 'our neighbors.' But it also warned, 'We cannot continue to allow people to enter the United States undetected, undocumented, and unchecked,' adding that 'those who enter our country's borders illegally, and those who employ them, disrespect the rule of the law.' By 2016, such language was gone."[6]

This embrace of the illegal and mass immigration comes at the expense of members of the American working class, who not only pay taxes to provide

★ ★ ★

Some Immigrants Are More Equal Than Others

Democrats aren't just promiscuously for all immigrants. Some immigrant populations are more useful in their electoral calculus—others, less so. In 2010, then–Representative Loretta Sanchez was running for reelection. Her district has a sizable Vietnamese community, along with a very large Hispanic population. Sanchez told Univision, "The Vietnamese and the Republicans are—with intensity—trying to take away this seat, this seat for which we have already done so much for our community." She accused her opponent of trying to take "this seat from us" and called him "very anti-immigrant and very anti-Hispanic." Her opponent's name was Van Tran. He is a Vietnamese immigrant. Van Tran accused Sanchez of going on a "racial rampage."[7] He was right. Imagine, if you will, a white Republican in a predominately white district talking about his black opponent taking "this seat from us." That might cause a ruckus, don't you think? But in the Hobbesean identity politics of post-American fragments clawing for power that is today's Democrat party, her slur went barely noticed.

public services to illegal aliens who work off the books but also lose job opportunities to low-skill migrants flooding the labor markets. And working class Americans have taken notice. That's why so many "blue" states flipped narrowly in 2016 to elect Donald Trump. In fact, Trump won the votes of millions of white blue-collar workers who had voted for Barack Obama. Henry Olsen wrote about this phenomenon in the *Los Angeles Times*:

> Surveys show that Obama-Trump blue-collar voters like Trump's anti-immigration stance. These voters are likely to have felt competition from immigrants legal and illegal, and they want that competition to stop. Even though many of these voters agree with Democrats on traditional economic issues like taxes and entitlement spending, their primary concern now is to protect

their livelihoods and standard of living by reducing competition from foreigners living at home and abroad.

Loud opposition to Trump's immigration policies reminds those voters every day why they no longer feel at home in today's Democratic Party.[8]

And before Democrats can clear their throats to call those white Obama voters racists, Democratic strategist and pollster Stanley Greenberg warns that many non-white Americans feel the same way. "The Democrats don't have a white working-class problem. They have a working-class problem," he said in a 2017 analysis of Democratic party voters. "Do not assume that African Americans do not share some of those concerns; many in our focus groups raise anxieties about competition from new immigrants."[9]

Those blue-collar voters aren't deluded. They see the situation on the ground, since they can't move to the gated communities where pumpkin latte liberals view immigration mainly as the source for new exotic takeout. Trump voters know that mass low-skill immigration is damaging to the American economy and American workers. But here's the thing that galls us: *So do many on the Left.* They have just ceased to care. Or else they've decided that the benefits of "diversity" are worth the damage to the most vulnerable Americans. You know, the way the Left in Russia back in the 1930s chose to collectivize all farms in Ukraine, sure that the short-term pain (mass famine) would be worth the long-term gain (a socialist utopia). Sometimes you have to destroy the working class in order to save it.

As Beinart has explained,

In 2005, a left-leaning blogger wrote, "Illegal immigration wreaks havoc economically, socially, and culturally; makes a mockery of the rule of law; and is disgraceful just on basic fairness grounds alone." In 2006, a liberal columnist wrote that "immigration reduces the wages of domestic workers who compete with immigrants" and that "the fiscal burden of low-wage immigrants is also pretty clear." His conclusion: "We'll need to reduce the inflow of low-skill immigrants." That same year, a Democratic senator wrote, "When I see Mexican flags waved at pro-immigration demonstrations, I sometimes feel a flush of patriotic resentment. When I'm forced to use a translator to communicate with the guy fixing my car, I feel a certain frustration."

The blogger was Glenn Greenwald. The columnist was Paul Krugman. The senator was Barack Obama.[10]

But that was before the memo went out that the new liberal plan for the American working class was planned obsolescence. Democratic politicians are now disenchanted with the American people, so they have decided to enfranchise a new one.

Labor Unions Manufacturing Dysfunction

You'd think labor unions would be the most vocal force against cheap (and often illegal) labor flooding into the country. As we discussed in chapter two, immigrants were used like sledgehammers against the growing labor movement. And labor unions hit back, strongly supporting the 1926 law reducing immigration. Union support for strong borders continued for decades and wasn't limited to white workers. Indeed, Latino icon and union organizer Cesar Chavez was a fervent backer of immigration laws. As Mark Krikorian explained in *National Review*,

Chavez fought illegal immigration tenaciously. In 1969, he marched to the Mexican border to protest farmers' use of illegal

aliens as strikebreakers. He was joined by Reverend Ralph Aber-
nathy and Senator Walter Mondale....

In the mid 1970s, he conducted the "Illegals Campaign" to
identify and report illegal workers, "an effort he deemed second in
importance only to the boycott" (of produce from non-unionized
farms), according to [Chavez biographer Miriam] Pawel. She quotes
a memo from Chavez that said, "If we can get the illegals out of
California, we will win the strike overnight." The Illegals Campaign didn't just report illegals to the (unresponsive) federal
authorities. Cesar sent his cousin, ex-con Manuel Chavez, down to
the border to set up a "wet line" (as in "wetbacks") to do the job the
Border Patrol wasn't being allowed to do.[11]

No more. Now virtually every labor union in America has jumped on
the pro–illegal immigrant bandwagon. Why? Well, the people who staff
and mostly run labor unions are not former factory workers. They tend to
be idealistic young leftists with prestigious college degrees, doing their
bit for "social justice." And people like that have mostly sloughed off the
patriotism of their grandparents and parents, trading it in for global
"solidarity." In addition, as manufacturing continues to be outsourced to
cheap-labor countries, the growth in labor organizations has shifted to
government employee unions, like the far-left Service Employees International Union (SEIU). Want to know that group's politics? It was one of
the first organizers of the anarchist- and Marxist-dominated Occupy Wall
Street demonstrations.[12] It is the SEIU that organizes the government
workers who staff bureaucracies—including the millions who serve the
massive social welfare programs from which poor immigrants benefit,
and for which they reliably (and sometimes even legally) vote at every
election. So the growing part of the labor movement is helping to create
jobs for its members by stoking the social dysfunction that comes from

importing poverty, "diversity," and ever bigger government.

The energy behind unions used to come from the men and women who went into the mines, built the cars, and poured the cement. It's now coming from those who pour the red ink. The hard hats have given way to the paper pushers.

It doesn't help matters to have the head of the

★ ★ ★

Is It Still the *American* Federation of Labor?

Even money says that the "A" is removed from AFL-CIO within five years. It's just not inclusive enough.

AFL-CIO on board with socialism. Richard L. Trumka essentially admitted in 2010 that he's not in it for the American worker: "I got into the labor movement not because I wanted to negotiate wages. I got into the labor movement because I saw it as a vehicle to do massive social change...."[13] In 2014 he promised illegal immigration advocates that his AFL-CIO would fight to stem deportations so immigrants could stop "feeling like your community is under attack, under siege all the time."[14]

Filling Pews, Virtue-Signaling, and Making George Soros Happy

We have already addressed the relevance of Christian faith to the immigration debate. As Christians, we should not be imposing via the coercive power of the state any law or policy that we can't argue for entirely based on natural law and justice. Take the abortion issue, for instance. Abortion is wrong not because it's un-Christian but because it kills the innocent, and the natural law written on everyone's heart tells us that's wrong. Amish Americans may personally be pacifists, but they don't enter politics and try to convince other Americans that our nation should disband its armed forces.

As Christians we can and should care for immigrants—in our own churches and with our own money. But we can't corral all America's Jews,

★ ★ ★

There's a Nuanced Analysis for You

We all remember how in 2016 Pope Francis called Donald Trump "un-Christian" for wanting to build a border wall. (That statement was issued from behind the Vatican's walls, in a city-state with fewer than two hundred citizens.) Three years earlier, speaking on Lampedusa, a tiny Italian island whose impoverished natives are swamped by economic migrants from Africa, Pope Francis had denounced those who wished to stem the immigrant flow, comparing them to . . . Cain, who murdered his brother, and King Herod, who slaughtered the infants of Bethlehem in an effort to snuff out Jesus.[15]

secularists, and others to back a Christian policy that cannot be justified by appeals to reason and natural law.

Not to worry, because the leftist policies promoted by open-borders churchmen aren't even Christian. They're post-Christian humanitarian mush. Lefty church activists posit limitless rights without responsibilities and demand that we close our minds to long-term, predictable, and catastrophic consequences for innocent third parties—like the rise of Islamist terrorism in Europe and cartel-linked gang crime in the United States.

The Bishops' Manifesto

In February 2017, twenty-four U.S. Catholic bishops joined a Vatican cardinal, Peter Turkson, for a conference in Modesto, California, sponsored by PICO—a Latin American leftist group heavily funded by atheist pro-choice leftist billionaire George Soros.[16] The "First U.S. Regional Meeting of Popular Movements" included not just the cardinal and the bishops, but staff from the Vatican department for the Promotion of Integral Human Development and the Catholic Campaign for Human Development (CCHD) as well.

The CCHD is the organization that radical Saul Alinsky personally helped left-wing Catholics to design. The Chicago branch of the CCHD, with the approval of then–Cardinal Joseph Bernardin, cut the check that sent the young Barack Obama to his first Saul Alinsky "community organizing" school.[17]

The "Messsage from Modesto" that the bishops endorsed calls for policies at the extreme Left of the political spectrum.[18] It claims that

- *[E]very human is sacred with equal claim to safe water, education, health care, housing and family-sustaining jobs.*

But the authors say nothing about freedom or private property rights. Apparently an "equal claim" means "a claim to equal" education, health care, and so forth. If every person on earth deserves the same level of all these scarce goods, it's the job of the government and the United Nations to equalize the wealth. Here in America, that means Catholic support for Obamacare, the further leveling down of education, a much higher minimum wage, and more aggressive federal colonization of middle class neighborhoods with low-income housing. The Message also states that

- *Our economy is meant to be in service of people, not profit.*

Okay, strictly speaking this is meaningless, so it's impossible to critique it. To the extent that this misty-eyed rhetoric gropes at something real, it is socialism, which five popes have condemned because it destroys the lives and freedom of "people," as it's doing right now in Venezuela.

- *Racism and all forms of human hierarchy, whether based on skin color, gender, sexual orientation, physical ability, arrest and conviction records, immigration status, religion or ethnicity are immoral.*

So every form of distinction we make among people is equally as evil as racism. It's sinful to distinguish at the polling place between illegal aliens and legal voting citizens; in hiring between murderers and veterans; in seminary admissions between gay and straight men.

> • *The lack of good jobs, affordable housing and clean water and air is literally killing people. Racism is stripping Black, Latino, Asian, Muslim and Native people of their humanity and fueling police abuse and mass incarceration, and fueling a crisis of homelessness and displacement. Raids and Trump Administration Executive Orders are scapegoating immigrants and ripping families apart.*

Does this seem to you like a fair description of life in today's America? Why do millions of people want to leave countries like Mexico and risk their lives to illegally enter such a dystopian nightmare society? If the countries they're leaving are even worse, why does this Message say nothing about the far worse injustices there? Really, all that matters to the authors is to promote the supposed right of illegal immigrants to stay in the United States no matter what. Or else we're "ripping families apart."

> • *[A] small elite is growing wealthy and powerful off the suffering of our families. Racism and White Supremacy are America's original sins. They continue to justify a system of unregulated capitalism that idolizes wealth accumulation over human needs.*

The only elite that really profits from illegal immigration is that composed of stockholders in companies that exploit their labor—and who strongly oppose Trump's efforts to enforce our laws. But the authors of this statement couldn't be bothered to know that. They don't even know that American capitalism is so hobbled and harassed that our country has dropped to number seventeen on the Index of Economic Freedom, its lowest ranking ever.[19]

But now we reach the point in the Message where Bluto (of *Animal House*) says, "We didn't give up when the Germans bombed Pearl Harbor!" and Pinto waves off the error: "He's on a roll."

- *The system's gangrene cannot be whitewashed forever because sooner or later the stench becomes too strong; and when it can no longer be denied, the same power that spawned this state of affairs sets about manipulating fear, insecurity, quarrels, and even people's justified indignation, in order to shift the responsibility for all these ills onto a "non-neighbor."*

That last pearl of wisdom isn't from Fidel Castro or Black Lives Matter. It's from a message of support that Pope Francis sent to the attendees of the Modesto meeting.

Next come the hard-headed policy proposals, where the authors scrupulously and calmly applied their dispassionate moral analysis, seeking the most prudent way to apply the moral principles they had asserted without violating people's rights or disrupting public order. Right?

No, of course not. Next comes the section where they grandstand and promise to cooperate with destructive radicals in flouting American law:

- *We urge every faith community, including every Catholic parish, to declare themselves a sanctuary for people facing deportation.... All cities, counties and states should adopt policies that get ICE out of our schools, courts and jails, stop handing over people to ICE....*

- *We must put our bodies, money and institutional power at risk to protect our families and communities, using tools that include boycotts, strikes, and non-violent civil disobedience. As Bishop Robert McElroy said to us, "We must disrupt those who would seek to send troops into our communities to deport the undocumented, to destroy our families. We must disrupt those who portray refugees as enemies. We must disrupt those who train us to see Muslim men & women as a source of threat rather than children of God. We must disrupt those who would take away healthcare, who would take food from our children.*

- *We ask our Catholic Bishops to write a covenant that spells out specific actions that dioceses and parishes should take to protect families in the areas of immigration, racism, jobs, housing and the environment.*

- *We propose to develop a shared curriculum and popular education program to equip people with analysis and tools to transform the world. We will focus on the development and leadership of young people. We will draw on the wisdom of our faith and cultural traditions, including Catholic Social Teaching. We recognize that our spiritual and political selves are inseparable. We have a moral obligation to confront and disrupt injustice.*

- *To defend our families and protect our values we must build political power. We must change the electorate to reflect our communities, through massive efforts to reach out to tens of millions of voters who are ignored and taken for granted by candidates and parties. We must hold elected officials accountable to the common good and encourage people in our communities to take leadership themselves, including running for office, so that we can govern the communities in which we live.[20]*

Do the cardinal and all those U.S. bishops and Vatican officials endorse the Message's sentiments as authentic Christian statesmanship? As sophisticated moral counsel? As a prudent means to obey Jesus' command to "Render unto Caesar what is Caesar's?"

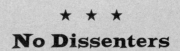

★ ★ ★

No Dissenters

Even the house "conservative" U.S. Catholic bishop Charles Chaput of Philadelphia routinely denounces virtually every attempt to enforce U.S. immigration laws.[21]

What's asserted in the Message from Modesto is madness, plain and simple. It is shrill, moralistic nonsense you might expect from an angry teenager who'd been reading Marxist websites and going through hormone surges. But the U.S. Bishops Conference, so many of whose members took part in the conference, said not a word distancing itself from this farrago. Instead, bishops ramped up their activism against Trump's immigration proposals.

The Bannon Challenge and the Bishops' Seedy Motives

Is moral hysteria the only reason for the bishops' almost unanimous embrace of de facto open borders? No, there are some hard-headed, real-world motives—that former White House chief strategist Steve Bannon was impolitic enough to talk about on television.

Bannon, a Catholic, offered a theory as to why the bishops ignore the Church's official teaching—which, as we have seen, in the official Catechism reads much like the GOP 2016 platform on immigration. Bannon told Charlie Rose on *60 Minutes*:

> The bishops have been terrible about this. By the way, you know why? You know why? Because unable to really—to—to—to come

to grips with the problems in the church, they need illegal aliens, they need illegal aliens to fill the churches. That's—it's obvious on the face of it. That's what—the entire Catholic bishops condemn [Trump].... They have—they have an economic interest. They have an economic interest in unlimited immigration, unlimited illegal immigration. And as much...as I respect Cardinal Dolan and the bishops on doctrine, this is not doctrine. This is not doctrine at all. I totally respect the pope and I totally respect the Catholic bishops and cardinals on doctrine. This is not about doctrine. This is about the sovereignty of a nation. And in that regard, they're just another guy with an opinion.[22]

New York's Cardinal Dolan went on Sirius XM to reply:

I don't really wanna care to go into what I think is a preposterous and rather insulting statement that the only reason we bishops care for immigrants is for the economic because we want to fill our churches and get more money. That's insulting and that's just so ridiculous that it doesn't merit a comment.[23]

Not exactly a detailed refutation, is it? In fact, it sounds a bit like a heated denial of a deeply uncomfortable truth. Along the lines of *Well, of course the emperor's not naked. Who could suggest such a preposterous and insulting thing? It's ridiculous.*

We don't think Cardinal Dolan is a venal or Machiavellian churchman. Neither does Steve Bannon. But we do think that he and the other bishops are *human.* God doesn't promise to guide the Church in its managerial decisions or political opinions. Nope, that's totally subject to the same fallen human nature that goaded Renaissance cardinals, Jimmy Swaggart, and the Reverend Jesse Jackson. We are all stuck with it too.

In *The City of God* St. Augustine taught us to analyze human actions with original sin in mind. (He compared the founders of Rome to a band of pirates.) That includes the actions of bishops, even popes. Like all of us they are subject to temptations from the devil. We are each of us drawn to the path of least resistance, to seek out praise and avoid public scorn. We're each of us tempted at times to "phone it in" instead of shouldering the cross.

So we should avoid the easy temptation to scapegoat illegal immigrants for our country's social problems. Agreed. That's something the bishops talk about a lot. It's popular with liberal journalists, so those statements get praised as courageous and quoted against Republicans by reporters who would march on Christmas morning to keep third trimester abortion for sex selection legal and taxpayer-funded.

But what should the bishops watch out for? What temptations come with the territory where they live?

Here we see that Steve Bannon has touched a very sore place in American Catholic life and leadership. According to Pew, some 40 percent of native-born Catholics formally leave the Church.[24] If it weren't for large-scale immigration from countries where bishops are better at preaching the faith than they are in the United States, the American Catholic Church would be shrinking at a rate comparable to the mainline Protestant denominations. One in four American Catholics today is an immigrant, most from Latin America.[25] And a disturbingly high percentage of immigrant Catholics leave the Church too, after a few years of life in tepid U.S. parishes.[26]

If you were a bishop and you looked at the flat or shrinking numbers of Catholics in your diocese, what would you think? Would you be eager to see the federal government cut into them still further by enforcing immigration laws? Or might you be tempted to echo the leftist line that those laws are somehow unjust?

And there's another benefit to lining up with the liberals on immigration: you can deflect the charge that you're a hardline conservative for opposing abortion and same-sex marriage. A pro-immigration message is one of the few things you can say in public that will absolutely get you praise in the secular press. That helps with donors, whose money you need for a thousand valid reasons. Like feeding the poor, and running pro-life pregnancy centers.

Speaking of money, that could be another temptation. Many Catholic institutions, including Catholic Charities, are so heavily funded by U.S. government grants—including very large grants to provide services to immigrants—that they are as much federal contractors as Christian apostolates. In 2014, the USCCB admitted that 97 percent of its spending on refugees was funded by the taxpayer.[27] This dependence on the feds has threatened Catholic institutions' freedom to follow Catholic teaching, for instance when dealing with "transgender" refugees.

If you were a bishop, would you want to see the budgets of your charities shrink by millions of dollars every year? Would you enjoy laying off good people because you don't have the money to pay them? Would the prospect of closing apostolates appeal to you? Probably not. So you might be tempted to support the government policies that spare you and your people all that pain.

It's only human.

To make this even clearer, imagine: Your doctor tells you that you really must lose some weight. It's key for your health. There are two routes you can take. Each seems like it would work. You can fiercely limit your calories and train for your local marathon. Or you can take a nice diet pill, which the government offers to send you for free. Which would be more attractive?

Add on these conditions. Imagine that the media and other elites scorned diet and exercise. That waiters openly mocked those who ordered salads in restaurants. That passersby pelted joggers with garbage.

Now what choice would you really prefer to make? That's the dilemma facing Catholic bishops.

Because there is another way to stop the Catholic population from hemorrhaging, to fill up your parishes and seminaries. But it's a stark and lonely road that wins you no "attaboys." In fact, it will get you mocked and spat on.

The signs on that road read "Orthodoxy" and "Tradition." And a few bishops are taking it. They are leading the revitalization of faithful Catholicism in their dioceses. They are cleaning the liberals out of the seminaries. They're insisting on orthodoxy in their parishes and schools. And they're seeing a surge of vocations, conversions, and Mass attendance. They're also under savage fire from the secular world and liberals within the Church's institutions. See what happened to Bishop Thomas Paprocki of Springfield, Illinois. All he did was to say that people in same-sex relationships couldn't receive Holy Communion. Seems obvious from a Catholic point of view. But the media painted him as if he'd joined the Ku Klux Klan. Even liberal Catholics joined the lynch mob.[28]

To be a faithful bishop with a thriving church, you'd have to take a thousand such difficult stands every year. Or you could keep the numbers up by just sitting back, letting the seminaries stay empty (or turn lavender) and waiting for new Catholics to show up from Latin America. And the public would praise you. Again, be honest: which would Screwtape tempt you to choose?

So Steve Bannon acted as a faithful Catholic laymen in calling on his bishops to wean themselves away from their debilitating addiction to immigration as a substitute for preaching and teaching the gospel. For that alone, he deserves a papal medal. (Maybe under the next pope.)

The Bible Says...

Some immigrant advocates point to Scripture. They quote Leviticus 19:33–34: "And if a stranger sojourn with thee in your land, ye shall not vex him. But the stranger that dwelleth with you shall be unto you as one born among you, and thou shalt love him as thyself."

Or Deuteronomy 27:19: "Cursed be he that perverteth the judgment of the stranger, fatherless, and widow."[29]

Indeed, we must take very seriously that both Old and New Testaments command us to welcome the stranger. As Brennan Breed, assistant professor of Old Testament at Columbia Theological Seminary, points out in the Huffington Post, "hospitality to the vulnerable makes ancient Israel stand out in stark relief from its neighbors."[30]

But Breed seems to think that God's command to love the stranger means letting in all comers regardless of the physical, social, or economic dangers they may pose. Or that the government has no say on who is let in and what rights they're granted.

Where those citing the Bible go astray is in missing the subtlety of the biblical Hebrew. Check out an article by James K. Hoffmeier, professor of Old Testament and Near Eastern Archeology at Trinity International University called "The Use and Abuse of the Bible in the Immigration Debate."[31] The Hebrew word translated as "the stranger" in the Scripture verses above is "*ger.*" *Ger* does indeed mean "alien" or "stranger," but it means one who has obtained legal status. Hebrew has other words for foreigner: *nekhar* and *zar.* The distinction is crucial.

Once the *ger* had been given legal status, certain rights and benefits were granted. And that is where equality kicked in. In Numbers 15:15 we read, "One ordinance shall be both for you of the congregation, and also for the stranger that sojourneth with you." We do. It's called the Constitution. It's why justice in this country is supposed to wear a blindfold.

There is a huge difference between an immigrant with legal status being denied equal justice (for example, the police not investigating if he gets robbed) and an immigrant being expected to follow our immigration laws and procedures before he is granted all the rights, privileges, and goodies of legal residency and citizenship. The first is an injustice that violates God's commands in the Bible. The second is prudence.

We can argue of those in the Church who wink at illegal crossings, who encourage refugees to abandon their culture and region to come here rather

★ ★ ★

Rent an Evangelical

Conservative Protestant groups have been targeted by George Soros and his legions of paid staffers, who have admitted in private documents to "renting" evangelical leaders as "mascots" to promote leftist policies such as open borders, using biblical arguments.[32]

Millions of dollars sluice behind the scenes to front organizations such as the Evangelical Immigration Table. As Juicy Ecumenism reports, "Politics makes for strange bedfellows goes the old saying. The marriage between a group of Evangelical Christian organizers and George Soros has birthed a new organization called the Evangelical Immigration Table (EIT). EIT reportedly does not legally exist and is an arm of the George Soros–funded National Immigration Forum, which as a 'neutral third-party institution' facilitated EIT's $250,000 radio ad campaign urging Evangelicals to back mass legalization of illegal immigrants. So if the EIT is just a front, then what exactly is the National Immigration Forum? NIF received over three million dollars from Soros' Open Society Institute (OSI) in 2009–2010 alone, as well as one million dollars from the left-wing Ford Foundation. Furthermore, *Sojourners* is also a recipient of Soros' money, and their President and CEO, Jim Wallis, is prominent within EIT."[33] For a more faithfully biblical read on immigration policy, follow Evangelicals for Biblical Immigration.

than stay in a safe haven near home, who remain silent as women and girls are sexually brutalized on their road to America, who cheer sanctuary cities where criminals can prey on those in the immigrant community, that *they* are the ones perverting the justice due the stranger.

Big Business Wants Cheap Labor

The 2016 GOP platform on immigration was clear and unequivocal: "America's immigration policy must serve the national interest of the United States, and the interests of American workers must be protected over the claims of foreign nationals seeking the same jobs."[34] Believe it or not, this position is controversial in high-dollar Republican circles. Some Republicans are not so much conservative or even pro–free market as simply pro-business—or pro–short term growth at any price. And the policies of previous administrations of both parties have exacted quite a high price for the real but limited economic stimulus of cheap labor imported from abroad. As Pew reports, working and middle class wages have been effectively flat for a generation:

> after adjusting for inflation, today's average hourly wage has just about the same purchasing power as it did in 1979, following a long slide in the 1980s and early 1990s and bumpy, inconsistent growth since then. In fact, in real terms the average wage peaked more than 40 years ago.... What gains have been made, have gone to the upper income brackets. Since 2000, usual weekly wages have fallen 3.7% (in real terms) among workers in the lowest tenth of the earnings distribution, and 3% among the lowest quarter. But among people near the top of the distribution, real wages have risen 9.7%.[35]

You might remember from chapter one how mass immigration has turned out to be a government wealth redistribution plan—from the working class to the wealthier. Imagine a flight attendant who went through Coach and confiscated every passenger's peanuts to hand them out in First Class. That's how immigration works in America.

The Federation for American Immigration Reform (FAIR) marshals the facts, noting,

> Immigration has been outpacing job growth in the U.S. for decades and is a contributing factor to unemployment, wage erosion, and declining labor force participation. Between 2000 and 2014, two new immigrants were admitted to the United States for every new job that was created by our economy. Between 2007

and 2015, all net new jobs created by the U.S. economy were filled by immigrants, legal and illegal.

During the ten-year period between 2005 and 2015, large-scale immigration swelled the ranks of working age adults by 25 million, while the number of people employed in the U.S. grew by just 7 million.

For the first time since the Great Depression, the majority of American households fall outside the income range that defines them as middle class. This phenomenon is not just an economic one; it threatens long-term social stability in the United States.

There is no labor shortage in the United States. The U.S. labor force participation rate now stands at just 62.6% of the working age population. Among workers with less than a high school diploma, the participation rate is a mere 45.4%. For those with a high school degree, but no college participation rate is just 57%. That is the lowest it has been since the 1970s, before many women were fully integrated into the U.S. labor force. Some 90 million working age adults in the U.S. are not participating in the labor force. Even accounting for those who are remaining in school longer, or are stay-at-home parents by choice, there is still a huge untapped supply of workers in this country.

Lower skilled American workers have seen the sharpest declines in income. Since 1970, real income for the bottom 90% of workers in the U.S. has declined by 8%. Over the same period, the foreign born population has grown by 325%. While there are many factors that have contributed to this phenomenon, the influx of more than 50 million immigrants has skewed the law of supply and demand in favor of employers. The impact has been particularly hard on those in the bottom 20% of wage earners. Just between 2009 and 2014, they have experienced a 5.7% decline in wages.[36]

Who benefits the most from mass immigration? One way to get a clue is to see who lobbies hardest for expanding immigration numbers and special visas, but opposes the enforcement of existing immigration laws.

Breitbart News noted, "Open borders organizations and the cheap foreign labor industry have teamed up with tech giants to push amnesty for roughly 800,000 to potentially 3.3 million illegal aliens in the United States. The pro-immigration group called the Coalition for the American Dream seeks to lobby Congress to pass a widespread amnesty plan that would allow illegal aliens protected and eligible for the Obama-created Deferred Action for Childhood Arrivals (DACA) program to remain in the U.S."[37]

Prominent in this coalition are "varying open borders organizations such as Council for Global Immigration, the National Immigration Forum, and Facebook CEO Mark Zuckerberg's FWD.us." More telling, perhaps, are the major corporations who signed on.

"Big businesses and organizations that profit from the continued importation of cheap foreign labor, as well as illegal immigration, are also involved with the group." Breitbart supplied a list:

- National Association of Manufacturers
- U.S. Chamber of Commerce
- American Hotel and Lodging Association
- NRF's Chain Restaurant Division
- Marriot International
- General Motors
- Hilton
- Hyatt
- Cummins
- Best Buy
- Mars Incorporated
- Western Union
- Cisco
- Under Armour
- Levi Strauss & Co.
- IKEA
- Dropbox
- Univision
- Chobani

- United States Hispanic Chamber of Commerce
- Shutterstock
- General Assembly
- Consumer Technology Association

As Breitbart also reported, "The tech industry, seemingly the biggest advocates of amnesty, immigration, and cheap foreign labor, have also tied themselves to the open borders coalition" and gave a separate list of "tech giants" involved with coalition:

- Glassdoor
- Slack
- Airbnb
- Google
- Intel
- Microsoft
- Amazon
- Apple
- IBM
- Lyft
- PayPal[38]

Tech, agriculture, construction, hotels, and restaurants are just a few of the industries that enjoy the cheaper labor costs which immigrants, legal and otherwise, provide.

Let's focus on one of our favorite subjects: food.

When candidate Donald Trump talked about deporting all illegal immigrants, famed chef Anthony Bourdain told Sirius XM that "every restaurant in America would shut down" if his plan came to fruition.[39]

That's an exaggeration. But there's some truth behind it. A 2008 analysis from the Pew Hispanic Center found that 20 percent of all cooks in American restaurants were illegals. (And roughly one third of dishwashers.) We can't be really sure of the percentage, though because a 2013 study conducted by the National Restaurant Association and Immigration Works USA determined that just over 20 percent of restaurant operators were using E-Verify—the free, easy-to-use federal system for checking any applicant's legal right to work in the United States. (We bet you thought that was mandatory, didn't you? Nope.)[40]

At least in the short term, even legal immigration in these industries pushes down wages for Americans. As Helen Raleigh noted at The Federalist,

> Analysis from Harvard labor economist George Borjas shows that immigrants (both legal and illegal) from 1990 to 2010 reduced the average annual earnings of American workers by $1,396 in the short run. However, the downward pressure of wages caused by new immigrants doesn't impact the entire American workforce in the same way. Some American populations get hit worse than others, depending on the type of work and its requirements of education, skills, and experience.
>
> Borjas's analysis shows the less-educated and least-skilled population suffers the most negative impact in the short term when competing against immigrants for the low-paying, least-skilled occupations—such as fruit pickers and restaurant dish washers—and often loses out to immigrants.[41]

Procreation—One of Those Jobs Americans Won't Do?

Now, many economists will insist that, over the long term, any growth in U.S. population will boost economic growth. More consumers, more producers, and all that. But for Americans living paycheck to paycheck, that long term never seems to come. They can't afford to buy homes, pay tuition, or invest for their retirements. There aren't any good studies yet, but some part of the decline in the native-born U.S. marriage and birth rates is probably linked to the uselessness of (immigrant-crowded, multilingual) public schools and the flattening out of wages. No worries, though—those American kids who never got born can be replaced…by immigrants!

One way to make sure that a country collapses is to pretend that it doesn't matter whether its citizens are willing or able to have a decent number of children—or if they outsource that "dirty job" to recent or future immigrants. A government that acts as if human children were interchangeable production and consumption units and child-rearing were some grubby sweatshop industry will harm the prospects of parents who wish to have decent-sized families—and then will become addicted to immigration to fill in the gaps.

★ ★ ★
The Europeans Are Already There

For every missing German baby, import a Syrian. What could possibly go wrong?

No, we're not being alarmists. Our elites are already talking up immigration as a means of coping with the collapsing birthrate among native Americans. As former Congressman Tom Tancredo noted in *The Hill*: "Former President Clinton, campaigning for the Senate's 'Gang of Eight' amnesty bill in 2013, picked up the theme, saying that if Congress understood what the economic impact of the country's declining fertility rate would be, they would pass the bill 'because it's the only way to keep our country growing.' In another post-Trump scare piece, the [*Wall Street*] *Journal* laments that 'an aging population, the physically demanding nature of many blue-collar jobs and the trend toward pursuing college degrees compound the labor shortage.' However, as Sen. Tom Cotton (R-Ark.) responded, 'Higher wages for Americans are a feature, not a bug, of reducing levels of legal immigration!'"[42]

Amen.

CHAPTER FIVE

Fake Solutions to Real Problems

Fixing our broken immigration system is kind of like the weather. Everyone talks about it, but nobody ever does anything about it. This generation has lived through several loud, flashy attempts to fix the immigration system. We're going to talk about four.

The 1986 Amnesty

Ronald Reagan made two mistakes that provide us with two unshakable maxims to live by:

First, never co-star with a chimp. The chimp will always get better reviews.

Second, never, *ever*, sign a deal with the Democrats where they get what they want first, while your part of the payoff comes later. Chances are, you'll never see it.

The deal Reagan made was called the Immigration Reform and Control Act of 1986. And what an act it was. By 2006 even the *New York Times* was calling it "Failed Amnesty Legislation": "President Ronald Reagan signed that bill into law with great fanfare amid promises that it would grant legal status to illegal immigrants, crack down on employers who hired illegal workers, and secure the border once and for all. Instead, fraudulent applications tainted the process, many employers continued their illicit hiring practices, and illegal immigration surged."[1]

Once current workers got legal status, there was little motivation for employers to verify that new workers were legally in the country. Republicans in Congress eager to please big business donors joined liberals like Teddy Kennedy to gut the enforcement part of the deal.[2]

So there was plenty of motivation for illegals to continue coming. And with no increase in border security there was little to stop them.

And you thought the biggest flop in the '80s was New Coke.

In 1986, there were 3.2 illegal immigrants in the United States. In 2012, there were an estimated eleven million. A 1997 report by the Center for Immigration Studies indicated that the 1986 Amnesty displaced 1,872,000 American workers its first decade alone.

Mark Krikorian, executive director for CIS, called the 1986 Act a "con job," for which he spread the blame liberally. "I think there's lot of blame to go around and spread around for decades," he said.[3]

Senator Chuck Grassley, a major player in the 1986 effort, said "The 1986 bill was supposed to be a 3-legged stool—control of illegal immigration, a legalization program, and reform of legal immigration."[4]

Cut two legs off a stool, and you find yourself flat on your *tuchus*.

The Gang of 8

In 2013, four Democratic senators and four Republican senators huddled together to hammer out a bipartisan comprehensive immigration reform (CIR) bill. These senators became known as "The Gang of 8."

The senators playing for the Democrats: Robert Menendez (New Jersey), Michael F. Bennet (Colorado), Richard J. Durbin (Illinois), and minority leader Chuck Schumer (New York).

On the Republican team: Arizona's John McCain and Jeff Flake, Lindsey Graham of South Carolina, and Florida's young Marco Rubio.

The Gang of 8 plan had four major provisions—three of which wouldn't raise any eyebrows:

- Expanding and improving the employment verification (E-Verify) system for all employers to confirm employee work authorization
- Improved work visa options for low-skill workers. This would include a program especially for agricultural workers
- Reforming the business immigration system, focusing on two fronts. First, reducing current visa backlogs. Second, keeping the brightest of the bright who come here to study. Specifically, fast-tracking permanent residence for U.S. university graduates with advanced degrees in science, technology, engineering, and math. You don't need to be a science whiz to see the wisdom of that

★ ★ ★

Partners in Crime?

According to the dictionary, a "gang" is an "organized group of criminals." It's not fair to call a distinguished group of Senators criminals. Or at least not seven of the eight. Senator Robert Menendez barely avoided retrial on assorted bribery and corruption charges. But he still faces potential trouble in the Senate for his alleged procurement of underage hookers overseas.

It's the fourth provision that was the deal-breaker:

- A "path to citizenship" for illegal immigrants already in the United States

★ ★ ★

Little Marco Learns His Lesson

When Rubio ran for the GOP nomination in 2016, even he admitted his mistake and said that securing the border must come first. Maybe he would have had better luck turning his new position into a mantra: "Build the Wall." Never mind. Someone else beat him to it.

There's another word for that: amnesty. The Gang of 8 made this gracious gift contingent on certain border security and visa-tracking improvements. (Well, maybe not so "certain." The Reagan Amnesty showed us that.) The plan did put these illegals at the back of the line. They would only be offered permanent status after legal immigrants already in line had been given permanent status. Of course, this only crowds out or delays those countless others hoping to get in line the proper way.[5]

Besides creating a "pathway to citizen-ship"—in other words, amnesty—for the esti-mated eleven million illegal immigrants here, the Gang of 8 plan also created hernias. The original bill was 844 pages long, and it grew to 1,200 pages after amendments, including attempts at stronger border security measures, were added.[6]

Remembering the lesson of 1986, the GOP, particularly in the House, wanted no part of what was essentially an amnesty with no rock-solid effort to secure the border first. Then, in June 2014, any hope the House would act on comprehensive immigration reform went out the window when immigration advocate House Majority Leader Eric Cantor of Virginia got his clock cleaned in his Republican primary by conservative ingénue and dark-horse Dave Brat. Immigration wasn't the only reason Cantor was kicked out on his caboose. But it was enough of a factor to scare Republicans away from any more sellouts, for a season.

It didn't help matters for the Gang of 8 when in May and June of 2014 tens of thousands of unaccompanied children illegally flooded across the Mex-ican border, creating a humanitarian crisis.[7]

DACA and the Dreamers

How many times did President Barack Obama say that executive action to protect the so-called Dreamers would be unconstitutional? "Our system doesn't work like that," he'd say, or it was "not an option"? At least three times.[8] (It only takes three times saying his name to summon Beetlejuice.)

Yet that is precisely what Obama ultimately did, circumventing Congress to conjure up DACA—or Deferred Action for Childhood Arrivals. He used what he claimed was his executive authority to suspend the deportations of young immigrants brought to the country illegally by their parents. And he did it against the expressed will of the United States Congress.

Same with Obama's 2014 DAPA action, or Deferred Action for Parents of Americans. Courts declared that one unconstitutional—as they would have DACA if they had gotten the chance—but Trump suspended it first.

Obama's antics would have made the Founders flip their powdered wigs.

Obama created whole new massive benefits for two classes of illegal immigrants. The Obama administration tried the argument that he was only offering "guidance." But Obama himself said when he was announcing the program, "I just took an action to change the law."[9] As law professor Jonathan Turley said, "If a president can claim sweeping discretion to suspend key federal laws, the entire legislative process becomes little more than a pretense."[10] Barack Obama treated the Constitution like one of his old Chum Gang joints. He lit it, smoked it, and basked in the buzz and the thrill of not being busted for it.

Obama's DACA decree served as a starting whistle for that flock of tens of thousands of Central American children caught racing across the border in 2014. Or so said Trump administration Attorney General Jeff Sessions. DACA "contributed to a surge of unaccompanied minors on the southern border that yielded terrible humanitarian consequences." Also, said Sessions, since most DACA beneficiaries are now adults, Obama "also denied jobs to hundreds of thousands of Americans by allowing those same jobs to go to illegal aliens."[11]

★ ★ ★
End It or Mend It?

In 2017, President Trump announced that he was going to let DACA expire. But. There was a big "but." He also said he was open to Congress passing a legit version of DACA for the Dreamers. He gave them six months. In September, Trump and the Democrats looked like they were closing in on a deal.[12] In October, Trump issued a list of "principles" he said must be part of any deal. They included funding for the border wall, thousands of more immigration officers, and a crackdown on those unaccompanied minors from Central America. Nancy Pelosi and Chuck Schumer immediately rejected the list and declared a deal off the table.[13]

As of this writing, the haggling continues.

Before we go into our own proposed solution for America's immigration problems—laid out in the next chapter—we want to put on our Hammer Pants and jump back into the '90s. There we find American icon Barbara Jordan, Democratic Congresswoman from Texas.

Barbara Jordan and the U.S. Commission on Immigration Reform

Barbara Jordan first came to national fame for her measured wisdom during the Watergate crisis. Her voice during those endless, dispiriting hearings resonated with integrity and commanded respect. As Texas journalist Molly Ivins put it, "We always said that if Hollywood ever needed somebody to play God Almighty, they ought to get Barbara Jordan."[14]

In 1993, Bill Clinton put Representative Jordan in charge of the U.S. Commission on Immigration Reform. She worked on the issue for two years before her tragic premature death. Much of what Jordan said and suggested while working on the Commission we can take to heart as we move forward toward a solution.

Top in Jordan's mind was the patriotic goal of Americanization. But let's let her do her own talking:

On Americanization: "[I]mmigration to the United States should be understood as a privilege, not a right. Immigration carries with it obligations to embrace the common core of the American civic culture, to seek to become able to communicate—to the extent possible—in English with other citizens and residents, and to adapt to fundamental constitutional principles and democratic institutions."

Limits on Immigration: "As a nation of immigrants committed to the rule of law, this country must set limits on who can enter and back up these limits with effective enforcement of our immigration law."

Skilled over Unskilled, and No Chain Migration: "Unless there is a compelling national interest to do otherwise, immigrants should be chosen on the basis of the skills they contribute to the U.S. economy. The Commission believes that admission of nuclear family members and refugees provide such a compelling national interest, even if they are low-skilled. Reunification of adult children and siblings of adult citizens solely because of their family relationship is not as compelling."

Protect American Workers, Particularly the Most Vulnerable: "Immigration policy must protect U.S. workers against unfair competition from foreign workers, with an appropriately higher level of protection to the most vulnerable in our society."

Stop Illegal Immigration: "To make sense about the national interest in immigration, it is necessary to make distinctions between those who obey the law, and those who violate it. Therefore, we disagree, also, with those who label our efforts to control illegal immigration as somehow inherently anti-immigrant. Unlawful immigration is unacceptable."

No Illegal Immigrants at the Public Trough: "Illegal aliens have no right to be in this country. They are not part of our social community. There is no intention that they integrate. As human beings, they have certain rights— we certainly should not turn them away in a medical emergency. As a nation, it is in our interest to provide a limited range of other services— immunizations and treatment of communicable diseases certainly fall into that category. But, if illegal aliens require other aid, it should rightly be provided in their own countries...."

★ ★ ★

Another Ally in the Effort for Smarter Immigration: NumbersUSA

NumbersUSA describes itself as the nation's largest grassroots immigration-reduction organization and claims eight million participants in all 435 congressional districts.

Founder and President Roy Beck believes "the key factor in immigration policy is choosing the right number of authorized immigrants for future years. To choose a lower number does not imply anything negative about the immigrants who already are legally in this country. We're talking about the future number that is best for both U.S.-born and foreign-born citizens."

The organization lobbies public officials in support of immigration policies that "protect all Americans—especially the most vulnerable and including the foreign born—from losing wages, individual freedoms, quality of life, and access to nature due to excessive immigration numbers that indiscriminately enlarge the U.S. population, the labor force and government costs."

NumbersUSA was founded to promote the recommendations of the U.S. Commission on Immigration Reform, chaired by Barbara Jordan, and of and President Bill Clinton's Task Force on Population and Consumption.[15]

Despite being inspired by the work of Democrats, NumbersUSA is naturally in the crosshairs of the Southern Poverty Law Center.[16]

"There are people who argue that some illegal aliens contribute to our community because they may work, pay taxes, send their children to our schools, and in all respects except one, obey the law. Let me be clear: that is not enough."

Refugees Are Often Better Off Closer to Home: "Certain legal immigrant populations may impose other costs: refugees often have special needs for health and other services, making resettlement significantly more costly than overseas solutions to refugee problems."

Principles for Immigration Reform: "Credibility in immigration policy can be summed up in one sentence: those who should get in, get in; those who should be kept out, are kept out; and those who should not be here will be required to leave."[17]

Yes, believe it or not, that was a Democrat talking.

Speaking at the Democratic National Convention in 1976, Barbara Jordan said, "A spirit of harmony will survive in America only if each of us remembers that we share a common destiny; if each of us remembers, when bitterness and self-interest seem to prevail, that we share a common destiny."

Hamilton, Jefferson, or Washington could not have said it better.

But harmony is the last thing on the minds of progressives today. They consider words like "Americanization" offensive. Micro-aggressions. Hate speech.

So a real solution to our immigration program is not only more difficult than it was twenty years ago. It must, by necessity, be more restrictive.

It is to that solution that we now turn.

CHAPTER SIX

MISSION America

W e've spent a lot of time in this book recounting the problems posed by our current immigration system, and indicting those who profit from the corrupt, chaotic status quo. But if we aren't going to offer what we believe is a fair, workable, humane, and sane program to solve our nation's immigration woes, then we're nothing more than whiners. In fact, while the solutions are as complex as the problem, they are also clear. They're fair. They're grounded in sound, just principles, not blind sentiment or exaggerated fears. They grow out of solid precedents in prudent historic policy. The outcome they promise is an orderly, tolerant, fiscally sound nation that looks out for its most vulnerable citizens. Restoring such an order would do a lot to defuse ethnic tensions and deprive resurgent racialists of the fuel that feeds their movements.

We call our plan MISSION America, which stands for Managing Immigration to Strengthen and Secure Our Nation. If the Dreamers can have an acronym, so can we.

MISSION America is not a mission impossible. None of these policies would require radical changes in our law, or Constitutional amendments. What they do demand is the courage to stand up against the moralizing

Did you know?

★ The total cost of the Wall is less than half of what we spend educating illegal immigrants in one year

★ Over 700,000 foreign visitors to the United States in 2016 overstayed their visas

★ Non-citizens are only 9 percent of our population but 27 percent of federal prisoners

★ Trump is flipping the numbers of refugees we take from overwhelmingly Muslim to majority Christian

demagogues who bully anyone who dares to point out the problems in broken immigration system.

And nowadays, that's asking a lot.

The Fifteen Building Blocks of MISSION America:

1. **Build** the Wall.
2. **Track** those who enter the United States on visas and immediately remove those who overstay them.
3. **Strip** sanctuary cities of discretionary federal funding and use other means to exert pressure on them.
4. **Remove** criminal aliens first, including those who commit ID theft.
5. **Check** the right of new applicants to work legally in America via E-Verify, which must be mandatory for every business with five or more employees.
6. **Create** a federal hotline, like the IRS hotline, allowing citizens to report illegal immigrants to ICE for removal.
7. **Pass** a federal law that ends birthright citizenship to children of illegal immigrants, then fight for it in the courts.
8. **Stop** chain migration.
9. **End** the "Diversity Visa" lottery.
10. **Fix** legal immigration. We should favor highly skilled workers, with lower overall totals.
11. **Shrink** immigration admissions from high-risk countries to as close to zero as possible.
12. **Update** our citizenship oath to require renouncing "religious laws or systems of laws" that are contrary to the U.S. Constitution.

Then pass laws revoking citizenship for any naturalized person who took this oath and goes on to break it.

13. **Honor** the "first safe country" rule for refugees. Help resettle genuine refugees in compatible nearby countries. Require refugees to return to their home countries when it's safe.

14. **Enforce** the financial promises made by sponsors to prevent immigrants from becoming a public charge.

15. **Boost** broad-based public and private efforts to assimilate and Americanize immigrants.

Ideally, every step in MISSION America would be complete before we made any provision at all for offering legal residence to illegal immigrants now present in America. Since any amnesty offered would serve as a magnet to future illegals, it would be reckless and irresponsible to move in that direction until this comprehensive agenda is complete. And of course legal status should never be offered to those who have committed serious crimes, including identity theft. Our lawmakers must keep that in mind as they fend off deals offered by legislators with long track records of favoring amnesty, who offer a few enforcement provisions as sweeteners. Remember the 1986 Amnesty, and don't get fooled again.

Now we sweat some of the details. MISSION America puts safety first.

1. Build the Wall.

"Any nation worth its salt must control its borders," as Democratic congresswoman Barbara Jordan said.[1] To accomplish that we must secure our long southern border with Mexico. Instead of using "impassible" deserts as barriers, we should wall them off, to save immigrants from narco-traffickers and human smugglers who are willing to risk lives for a price.

We don't let strangers walk willy-nilly into our homes. We're not sure how Robert Frost meant the phrase, but good walls really do make good neighbors. Think of the difference between a suburban block with nice, secure homes, and a shelter where the homeless sleep on beds unsecured from strangers. Makes sense on a gut level, doesn't it?

With a Wall you don't have families sprinting across the 5 Freeway near San Diego, dodging cars. You won't know, in the back of your mind where you try to keep such unhappy thoughts, that thousands of Latino children every year are easy prey for coyotes and sexual predators. You will not see heavily-armed gang members and drug dealers making lives hell in border towns. We won't have the same quantity of drugs flooding into our neighborhoods, via the billion-dollar narco-cartels that control large portions of Mexico. We'll have to worry less about Islamic terrorists trying to sneak in weapons of mass destruction or suicide bombers. (One such effort was barely thwarted a few years after 9/11.)[2]

With a Wall you know who's coming through the door. If you need a ticket to get into a concert, you should need a ticket to get into the country.

With a Wall you control how many are coming in. We know the chaos when people crash a party. Why would we allow people to crash our country?

Border barriers are proven to reduce illegal immigration.[3] Ask former LA Mayor Antonio Villaraigosa. As Breitbart reported, the Democrat and second-generation Mexican-American "demanded an exception to zoning laws so he could build a six-foot high wall around his official residence."[4] And that's from a pol who's a long supporter of MEChA, a Hispanic separatist organization that encourages anti-American activities and civil disobedience.[5] (MEChA wants to reannex California to Mexico. We know...some days it's tempting to say "Go ahead, take it.")[6]

The Department of Homeland Security estimates the cost of a border Wall at $21.6 billion. Trump thinks he can do it for $10 billion.[7]

★ ★ ★

Another Ally in the Effort for Smarter Immigration: ACT for America

ACT for America's focus is on the threat from radical Islam. Claiming five hundred thousand members, ACT for America describes itself as the "largest national security grassroots organization in the U.S."

In its policy statement, ACT for America states, "Through our advocacy and activism, we will continue to address the threat presented by those who seek to destroy our Western way of life through advocating violence or radical religious discrimination through hate groups, such as those represented by movements like radical Islam."[8]

The organization was formed in 2007 by Brigitte Gabriel, who has become a familiar face on Fox News, CNN, and MSNBC debating the issues involving the rise of global Islamic terrorism and its threat to America.

But who's going to pay for our Wall? Maybe Trump's promise to make Mexico pay was just red meat for the campaign trail. The U.S. government would actually save billions by putting a Wall in place. The $21.6 billion figure isn't even half of what we spend each year just on educating illegal immigrants.[9]

Here's another idea: GoFundMe. That's right. Given the broad popularity of the Wall, Trump could announce that he's funding it via donations. How many Americans, frustrated with the loss of their country to chaos, would gladly contribute, perhaps in return for getting their name on a brick or section of the Wall?

One way or another, the Wall pays for itself.

But a Wall is only part of the solution.

2. Track those who enter the United States on visas and immediately remove those who overstay them.

Two-thirds of those in the "undocumented population did so by entering with a valid visa then overstaying their period of admission." This according to NBC News, citing the Center for Migration Studies (CMS)."[10] Senator Marco Rubio put the figure at 40 percent.[11] Whatever the percentage, visa abuse is clearly a gaping hole in our nation's security.

We must closely track all those who enter our country on visas and immediately remove those who overstay. First, the tracking. How hard can that be? We already have cellphone apps that can track family, friends, and wayward lovers.[12] Restaurants now text us when our table is ready. Certainly Homeland Security can warn those on visas when it's getting near time to go. If they don't report in by the deadline, they should be reported to local police as fugitives, arrested, and promptly returned to their home countries.

We have every right to know who is in our country. We have the right to demand that they follow our laws. According to Homeland Security, 1.5 percent of the 54 million who came to the United States on visas in 2016 overstayed. That's nearly 740,000 new illegals.[13] The Obama administration, predictably, ignored this problem. According to the *Washington Times*,[14] in 2015, just *2,500* visa overstays resulted in deportations. In the whole country.

We already know the risks that such lawlessness poses. Fifteen of nineteen of the hijackers who perpetrated the World Trade Center and Pentagon attacks on September 11, 2001, never should have been allowed in the United States. They only got in because of what ABC News called "staggering lapses" in the State Department's visa program. As we have seen, three of the terrorists were illegal overstays.[15] Had George W. Bush been comfortable with enforcing our country's immigration laws, he could have used that appalling fact to sell voters on the need to clean up the system. He didn't. It took the election of Donald Trump to offer a prayer of doing that.

3. Strip sanctuary cities of discretionary federal funding, and use other means to exert pressure on them.

Remember when harboring fugitives was a bad thing? More and more cities, from New York to San Francisco, are not only telling illegal immigrants to come. They are telling federal ICE agents to stay away. They are the so-called "sanctuary cities." It's an easy way for Democratic mayors to preen as defenders of "diversity"—and presumably win the votes of the illegal aliens' family members and co-nationals who have citizenship and can vote legally. Governor Jerry Brown has declared California a sanctuary state—a defiance of federal sovereignty not seen since... well, 1860.

When officials refuse to report illegal aliens to ICE, repeat offenders may be released to commit more crimes instead of being detained or deported. The editorial board of *USA Today*—not exactly known for conservative views—has opined that this policy "violates common sense."[16] Kate Steinle learned that the tragic way. Juan Francisco Lopez-Sanchez had been deported from the United States *five times*. He was on probation at the time of the shooting. He had *seven* felony convictions. ICE had a detainer out for him. But because of its "due process for all" sanctuary city policy, San Francisco let him go free—and Kate Steinle was shot dead.

Then, a San Francisco jury, in a middle finger to Trump, declared Lopez-Sanchez not guilty.[17]

Sanctuary cities attract illegal aliens. They're only human, like you and me. Why wouldn't people breaking a law cluster in places that promise to obstruct its enforcement? Of course, their presence increases the economic burden on a city. According to *National Review*, half of the forty-one million immigrants in the United States have settled in one of five metro areas: New York City-Newark, Los Angeles, Chicago, Miami, or San Francisco. What do these places have in common? All of them resist or obstruct the enforcement of our nation's immigration laws.

Cutting federal funding to cities that defy federal law will make it even more fiscally painful for those cities to continue flouting their Constitutional obligation to cooperate with our nation's central government. In the meantime, it will free up more federal money to help law enforcement in municipalities that still respect rule of law.

4. Remove criminal aliens first, including those who commit ID theft.

Here's one area where the lucid among us agree. We must make it a priority to deport criminal aliens. Discussing Government Accountability Office studies from 2005 and 2011 on criminal aliens who were incarcerated, the Heritage Foundation reported,

> The first report (GAO-05-337R) found that criminal aliens (both legal and illegal) make up 27 percent of all federal prisoners. Yet according to the Center for Immigration Studies, non-citizens are only about nine percent of the nation's adult population. Thus, judging by the numbers in federal prisons alone, non-citizens commit federal crimes at three times the rate of citizens.
>
> The findings in the second report (GAO-05-646R) are even more disturbing. This report looked at the criminal histories of 55,322 aliens that "entered the country illegally and were still illegally in the country at the time of their incarceration in federal or state prison or local jail during fiscal year 2003." Those 55,322 illegal aliens had been arrested 459,614 times, an average of 8.3 arrests per illegal alien, and had committed almost

700,000 criminal offenses, an average of roughly 12.7 offenses per illegal alien.[18]

Think of that: the average imprisoned illegal alien averaged nearly over a dozen offenses and had been arrested more than eight times. Only in America's dysfunctional immigration regime can you have eight strikes and still not be out.

And America still offers visas to the citizens of countries that won't take back their criminal aliens when we do get around to trying to deport them. How does that make sense? Is it anything but a vast "Kick Me" sign stuck on the back of the Statue of Liberty? The Trump administration is finally making progress on this front. The *Washington Times* reported, "Between cajoling, threats and actual punishments, Homeland Security has managed to drastically cut the number of countries that habitually refuse to take back immigrants whom the U.S. is trying to deport, officials said Tuesday, notching an early immigration success for President Trump.

"The number of recalcitrant countries has dropped from 20 to 12 over the months since the presidential election, and some longtime offenders—including Iraq and Somalia—have earned their way off the naughty list. The list of countries is the shortest this decade."[19]

Deporting rapists and killers is not a hard political sell. (Yet. Give the Left time.)

But we must go further. One of the most common crimes committed by illegal immigrants is identity theft. It harms millions of Americans, and those who engage in it deserve to be shown the door and banned from reentry to America. For life. As Joe Guzzardi reported in *USA Today*, "According to an audit by the Treasury Inspector General for Tax Administration, 1.4 million illegal aliens in 2015 used falsified or stolen Social Security Numbers to get hired.... The *Washington Times* reported that 87 percent of online tax submissions with an ITIN showed income associated with a Social Security Number which could not possibly belong to the filer."[20]

Identity theft is a felony. You can't say that an illegal alien is "law-abiding" if he is using someone else's stolen Social Security Number. And, as the Center for Immigration Studies observes, you can't even euphemistically call an illegal alien "undocumented" if he is walking around with fake documents.[21]

Identity theft by illegal aliens:

- Results in billions of dollars leaving the country from falsely documented workers getting paid and sending money home[22]
- Steals jobs from Americans
- Makes a mess of the lives and credit and tax situations of its victims
- Facilitates illegal aliens voting in our elections

Children are particular targets, says CIS: "Children do not use their SSNs for employment or to obtain credit so parents generally do not check their children's credit histories, allowing a person using a child's SSN to go undetected for years. Sometimes document vendors sell fraudulent identity packages using unassigned SSNs that are later assigned to children, causing them problems before they are even born."[23] For a galling take on just how absurdly easy it can be to get top-notch fake documents, see a 2004 *LA Times* article by Steve Lopez called "Not Legal but Need a License?"[24]

If a citizen commits identity theft, he can face fifteen years in prison.[25] Aggravated identity theft is punishable by a mandatory minimum sentence of two years.[26] An illegal who commits identity theft is treated about as seriously as a shoplifter.

Clearly we need to tighten up the process for issuing government documents. That's complex, involving each of the fifty states. So for a start, we should make the punishment for violating these laws a stiff one: we remove you from the country, and we never let you come back.

5. Check the right of new applicants to work legally in America via E-Verify, which must be mandatory for every business with five or more employees.

E-Verify is an Internet-based system that allows business to determine the eligibility of their employees to work in the United States.[27] It compares what a potential employee puts on his I-9 form with government data. According to DHS, six hundred thousand employers now use E-Verify, and they claim satisfaction with the system at a rate of 85 percent.[28]

But maddeningly, the use of E-Verify is voluntary in most of America. According to a 2012 survey by the Center for Immigration Studies, only sixteen states required the use of E-Verify in some form. A year earlier, California—the "sanctuary state"—passed an act to prohibit municipalities from mandating use of E-Verify![29] Other liberal bastions such as Illinois have also tried to limit the use of E-Verify.[30]

There is no sophisticated way to make an argument this obvious: Since it is illegal to work in the United States, *if you are here illegally*, it is a no-brainer to mandate the use of a successful system for confirming whether a potential employee is legal. It protects American workers, it protects employers, and it chokes

★ ★ ★
Not the Best Business Plan

A few years back, Al Perrotta and his wife, Rusty, came across the perfect fixtures for the bathroom they were remodeling. They called the company to order. The wait for the fixtures would be eighteen months. Why? They discovered that the company had been utilizing illegal workers, including their master craftsman. ICE raided the place, and the business was dead in the water. Dead of a self-inflicted wound. Another company, whose workers were legal, saw the opening and ramped up production of similar-looking fixtures—and business poured in like water.

off a major incentive for moving here illegally. We're flabbergasted that we even need to say any of this.

E-Verify. It works. It takes seconds. Less time than it takes to check your Twitter feed. A simple obvious fix. Ask yourself who benefits from not mandating E-Verify, and if they are looking out for what's best for Americans.

6. Create a federal hotline, like the IRS hotline, allowing citizens to report illegal immigrants to ICE for removal.

The IRS has a Tax Fraud Hotline that allows citizens to report tax cheats. Or rather, it allows citizens to call and order a form to detail the alleged tax fraud. You can't just call up anonymously and snitch on a neighbor.[31]

ICE needs a similar hotline to report immigration cheats. No, we can't have people just calling up and saying, "The guy mowing the grass across the street—I know, I just *know* he's illegal!" You're going to need to fill out a form, you're going to need to have evidence. This ICE Hotline would be particularly beneficial in nabbing businesses that are violating the law. It would offer companies that follow the law and hire legal workers some recourse against competitors who are putting them out of business by using illegal (uninsured, underpaid, unprotected, *exploited*) workers.

7. Pass a federal law that ends birthright citizenship for children of illegal immigrants, then fight for it in the courts.

If a pregnant woman en route from her native Indonesia to Iceland stops on a layover in Chicago, and gives birth in O'Hare Airport, her child is a U.S. citizen. When he turns twenty-one, he can petition for her to be admitted to the country, so she can eventually become a U.S. citizen too. Does that make sense to you?

We chose an outrageous, unlikely example, but things almost as absurd happen all the time. Pew estimates that 7.5 percent of all births in the United States—or about three hundred thousand every year—are to illegal immigrants.[32] Some eight thousand births each year are part of "birth tourism" typically to mothers from wealthier countries who travel to the United States specifically to give birth in America. But whether these babies' parents are rich tourists or poor Mexican agricultural laborers, these children become "anchor babies" whose U.S. citizenship allows other family members to jump the line for legal residency and U.S. citizenship. Anchor babies also qualify for generous welfare benefits.[33]

Outliers

According to the Center for Immigration Studies, the United States and Canada are the only two economically advanced nations that give citizenship to the offspring of illegal immigrants. Overall, only thirty of 194 countries do so.[34]

How did we get here? Thanks to a dubious reading of the 14th Amendment, which was ratified in 1868 in the wake of the Civil War. It reads: All persons born or naturalized in the United States, and subject to the jurisdiction thereof, are citizens of the United States and of the State wherein they reside." This is called the Citizenship Clause. It was meant as a crucial protection for freed slaves and their children. But our government turned it into a gift from Santa Claus to illegal immigrants.

Both the 14th Amendment and the Civil Rights Act of 1866 aimed to reject citizenship for those with only a temporary allegiance to United States or an allegiance to a foreign power. As Jon Feere of the Center for Immigration studies has written, "Opposition to granting citizenship to individuals subject to a foreign power was strong throughout the Senate. It does seem that the framers of the Citizenship Clause had no intention of establishing a universal rule of automatic birthright citizenship."[35]

As Feere notes, "The executive branch's current practice of extending birthright citizenship to nonresident aliens has never been authorized by any statute or any court decision." Opponents of birth citizenship for the children of illegals point to the phrase "and subject to the jurisdiction thereof." A child of illegals is not "subject" to the laws of the United States. That well-known right-wing xenophobe Sen. Harry Reid introduced legislation in 1993 that would have limited birthright citizenship to the children of U.S. citizens and legally resident aliens.[36] Others have proposed similar limitations in the years since.

The question is, would such a law pass muster with the Supreme Court? Why not find out? Especially since our court seems likely to move in a more originalist direction. Let's pass a law eliminating birthright citizenship going forward—grandfathering in every current U.S. citizen—and see how the Supreme Court rules.

8. Stop chain migration

Chain migration must end. Chain migration allows newly naturalized immigrants to bring in an unlimited number of foreign relatives to the United States with them. According to the Center for Immigration Studies, over 60 percent of all immigration in the United States is due to chain migration.[37] Others put the figure as high as 70 percent.[38]

Do the math. This immigration equivalent of "Red Rover, Red Rover, Send All My Relatives Over" creates an exponential increase in new arrivals. And again, they are brought in not on merit, but biology. What supporters call "Family Reunification."[39]

Somehow, the U.S. government has made itself responsible for unifying families that split apart on their own volition. (Who knows? Maybe we could pass a law making the government responsible for reuniting NSYNC.)

What's more, as already noted, the new arrivals tend to vote Democratic. The problem of chain migration is another reason the president should not give status to "Dreamers." The millions of future Democrats whom DACA and "Dreamer" illegals could invite here in future decades would seal the fate of the Republican party nationally and turn states like Texas purple, then blue.

President Trump is vowing to end chain migration. His vow took on extra urgency in the wake of an attempted bombing in New York City by a radicalized chain migrant.[40] A string of shootings targeting police officers in December 2017 in Harrisburg, Pennsylvania, was also carried out by a man who benefited from extended family chain migration. Said DHS, "The long chain of migration that led to the suspect's admission into the United States was initiated years ago by a distant relative of the suspect."[41]

The RAISE Act,[42] sponsored by Tom Cotton and David Perdue, would cut the long chain. It bases immigration on merit, skills, and English proficiency, rather than family ties.

The RAISE Act or similar legislation must pass. If we continue chain migration, the chain will become a noose.

9. End the "Diversity Visa" lottery.

America's current immigration system includes a "green card" visa lottery. Technically, it's called the Diversity Visa (DV) program. The name tells you a lot. Each year, fifty thousand people who want to emigrate are randomly selected to be given permanent resident visas. The idea is to diversify the U.S. immigrant population by selecting people from countries with low rates of immigration in the previous five years.

The first question to ask is, *Why do we even do this?* It's completely arbitrary, choosing immigrants based on no contribution they'd make to the country apart from showing up and adding "diversity." We're selecting people not on the content of their character but on their national origin. Judging them by their ethnicity, not their ability.

But worst of all, awarding U.S. residency (which leads to citizenship) this way degrades the value of U.S. citizenship to the status of *a prize in a lottery*.

The "diversity" isn't even all that diverse, if you think about it. Why diversity by nationality? Why not diversity by height? By hair color? Diversity by astrological birth sign? How long before some pagan complains we don't have enough Capricorns in America?

Hrishikesh Joshi, a postdoctoral research fellow at the University of Michigan, dove into this issue more seriously in an article for *The Hill*. Joshi noted that the lottery "rewards countries for being small. But why should this count as promoting diversity"? He explained that "it's just not true that all countries possess the same amount of 'diversity'—no matter how the notion of diversity is to be understood. Along any dimension of diversity—be it ethnic, cultural, religious, or linguistic—a country like Nigeria or Brazil is more diverse than a small, fairly homogenous country like Iceland."[43]

The terrorist who ran over and killed eight people in New York City in October 2017 entered the country via the Diversity Visa.[44] In his case, maybe, the pro–open borders crowd has a point. He did benefit the economy. After all, he rented the truck used in the terror attack.

10. Fix legal immigration. We should favor highly skilled workers, with lower overall totals.

Alabama Crimson Tide is the best of the best in college football. Each year they are in the hunt for the National Championship. They are elite. Many players from around the country, including a lot of very talented athletes, want to play for 'Bama. Alabama gets to pick and choose who among those hopefuls they bring onto the team—based on the needs of the team, each player's character, and his fit within the program.

If America wants a winning immigration program it should act like 'Bama. We must change our legal immigration system to favor highly skilled workers who fit the American team. We must take those who fill specific needs for our country. This is nothing new. This is precisely how our Founders saw the issue, as we laid out in chapter two.

Further, favoring highly skilled workers over low-skill—or for that matter no-skill—workers will mean that new arrivals aren't taking jobs from low-skill Americans, that our neediest fellow citizens aren't getting bumped off the bottom rungs of the ladder to success. What is the ultimate goal of any sane immigration policy? To strengthen America. Not to punish the weakest Americans.

The RAISE Act, introduced in 2016 by Senators Tom Cotton and David Perdue, would make an excellent start in that direction. As *National Review* noted, the act "would take a sledgehammer" to our current irrational system, "dramatically reducing low-skilled immigration and revamping our system for skilled immigration. It would cut immigration by more than 40 percent immediately, and by half in a decade.... It would end the diversity lottery and preferences for family members aside from spouses, minor children, and elderly parents in need of care. And it would put those seeking green cards on the basis of employment—140,000 of which would be available annually, the same number as today—through a new point system similar to those used in other developed countries."[45]

Let's hope that our legislators see the sense in proposals like this one.

11. Shrink immigration admissions from high-risk countries to as close to zero as possible.

The current Diversity Visa program, which liberals support, blocks people from a list of specific countries. Why? Not for any good reason, but just because those nations have *sent a high number of people* to the United States

★ ★ ★
Not Unprecedented

It is not as if cutting off immigration from high-risk countries were unheard of. FDR suspended Japanese and German immigration during World War II.[46] In 1980, well-known right-wing Islamaphobe Jimmy Carter banned Iranians after Iran seized our embassy.[47]

in the past five years. But when Donald Trump tried to block immigrants and visitors from nations teeming with extremists and terrorists, a national uproar ensued and judicial activists blocked his order—though it was clearly within his constitutional remit. That is how irrational our immigration system still is.

As the *Washington Times* reported, "The CIA said last year that the terrorist group's official strategy is to hide its operatives among refugees entering Europe and the United States via human flows out of the Middle East and North Africa. The Islamic State, also known as ISIL and ISIS, has inspired followers to commit atrocities in San Bernardino, California; Orlando, Florida; and the Fort Lauderdale airport in Florida. Scores of U.S. residents have been charged with or suspected of providing material support to the Islamic State. Some have left the U.S. to commit war crimes in Syria and Iraq."[48]

Why expose ourselves when we don't have to? Why let in huddled masses yearning to slit our throats?

A 2016 Senate study indicated at least seventy-two terrorists in the United States came from countries covered by President Trump's original vetting order. Further, notes the Center for Immigration Studies, the study showed that 380 of 580 people convicted in terrorist cases since 9/11 were foreign born. (The Senate report was compiled from open sources. The Obama Administration refused to provide government records. Never let your safety get in the way of the Left's agenda.)[49]

Look what's happening across the pond. Hungary's prime minister Viktor Orbán has called Europe's refugee policy the "Trojan horse of terrorism."[50] A little to the west, in Germany, Chancellor Angela Merkel flung open her borders to waves of unvettable Muslim migrants claiming to be refugees. She kicked off 2017 by declaring that her citizens could overcome the Islamist terror threat with more "openness." These remarks came just days after a jihadist slammed a truck into a Christmas market in Berlin, killing twelve. Germany is plagued with attacks from radical migrants. Meanwhile its police forces are prosecuting…online critics of Merkel's immigration policies. One couple in Bavaria was sentenced to prison and fines for opposing the influx of refugees,[51] and a German policeman was threatened with a fine of three months' wages for calling Merkel's policies "insane" at a public political rally.[52]

If you think that the Left won't try that in America, see how prosecutors are treating Christian bakers and florists who won't go along with same-sex marriage.

12. Update our citizenship oath to require renouncing "religious laws or systems of laws" contrary to the U.S. Constitution. Then pass laws revoking citizenship for any naturalized person who takes this oath and goes on to break it.

It's simple. Just like the one-time laws of the Inquisition, Sharia is incompatible with the U.S. Constitution. Anyone hoping to be a U.S. citizen cannot be loyal to both. As we showed in chapter two, when the mass influx of Catholics worried Protestant Americans whose ancestors had suffered under intolerant Catholic regimes, the United States updated its citizenship oath to make it clear that new Catholic Americans must not hold to Old World intolerant attitudes. Partly in response to these concerns, U.S. Catholic bishops went into overdrive asserting their attachment to religious freedom for all. Muslim leaders in the United States need to feel similar pressure to do the same. And Muslim immigrants to the United States need

A Book You're Not Supposed to Read

The Politically Incorrect Guide® to Jihad by William Kilpatrick (Regnery, 2016).

to know that there is no room whatsoever for Islamist supremacist movements in America.

Sharia is more than religious rules. It is a fully integrated forced marriage of religion and state. It is the Islamic system of morality and jurisprudence that governs all aspects of life. It's meant not just for Muslims, but for the whole world. It's a political ideology, centered on Muslims dominating society and enforcing Allah's rules of conduct on every human being, eradicating polytheists (such as Hindus), and forcing Jews and Christians into a position of silent subservience (dhimmitude). Islamic scripture and tradition command every Muslim to try to impose Sharia worldwide (though of course not all obey). The effort to do that is called jihad.

Former Muslim turned freedom activist Ayaan Hirsi Ali has this to say about the connection between Sharia, Islam, and Islamist political activism:

> Political Islam is not just a religion as most Western citizens recognize the term "religion," a faith; it is also a political ideology, a legal order, and in many ways also a military doctrine associated with the campaigns of the Prophet Muhammad. Political Islam rejects any kind of distinction between religion and politics, mosque and state. Political Islam even rejects the modern state in favor of a caliphate. My central argument is that political Islam implies a constitutional order fundamentally incompatible with the US Constitution and with the "constitution of liberty" that is the foundation of the American way of life. . . .
>
> The Islamists' program is fundamentally incompatible with the US Constitution, religious tolerance, the equality of men and

women, the tolerance of different sexual orientations, and other fundamental human rights.

The biggest challenge the United States faces in combating political Islam, however, is the extent to which agents of dawa can exploit the constitutional and legal protections that guarantee American citizens freedom of religion and freedom of speech—freedoms that would of course be swept away if the Islamists achieved their goals.[53]

Is it really unreasonable to ask potential citizens of the United States to renounce all that? Or for us to deport a naturalized person who later violates that oath? We deport other people who lie their way into our country—for instance, those who lied about their World War II records to hide their involvement with the Nazis.

13. Honor the "first safe country" rule for refugees. Help resettle genuine refugees in compatible nearby countries. Require refugees to return when it's safe.

What is a refugee? Someone fleeing his country to escape persecution. By international law, he is supposed to stop at the "first safe country" and remain there until it is safe for him to return home.[54] That's what "refuge" means—a temporary safe haven during an emergency. But our refugee program has been distorted out of any recognizable shape and turned into a stealth program for helping economic migrants resettle permanently in the United States, often on government benefits, as means of importing yet more "diversity." Because there really weren't enough Somali tribesmen in northern Maine before the 1990s. It's a good thing our government took care of that.

Nor were there sufficient young Muslim rapists in Sweden and Germany. Again, problem solved.

It's questionable how many of the million-plus Middle Easterners who poured through Turkey into Western Europe were even Syrians, much less actual refugees from that nation's civil war. What is clear is that the moment they left Turkey for greener pastures they ceased to be genuine refugees. Turkey (which had helped stoke that civil war) was a safe refuge for them. As Sunni Muslims, they were certainly in no danger of religious persecution. Turkey should have resettled them, in concert with other countries where these migrants could have assimilated more easily—such as rich, empty Saudi Arabia. However, the Saudis and other Gulf States took virtually zero refugees. Instead, they joined the propaganda campaign to resettle them in Europe and undertook to build them mosques and Muslim schools in cities like Paris and Berlin.[55]

This isn't refugee protection. It's colonization, along the lines of what England, France, and Spain did to the natives of the Americas.

A 2015 study by the Center for Immigration Studies showed that it costs twelve times as much to transport and resettle a Middle Eastern "refugee" in the United States as it would to put him up safely in the first safe country.[56] And if helping to save lives is what our government really has in mind, that is what it will do. We have ample leverage over Middle Eastern nations that swim in American military aid—like Saudi Arabia—to compel them to accept such refugees instead of wasting vast sums resettling them in American communities.

Now there are some categories of refugee for whom the "first safe country" might be America. Namely, Christians and other persecuted minorities in an increasingly intolerant Middle East. But those are precisely the people the United States has long ignored. As The Daily Caller documented, "Obama admitted more than 12,000 Muslim refugees from Syria in Fiscal Year 2016, but fewer than 100 Christian refugees from the same country. Christians make up about 10 percent of the population in Syria, some 2.2 million people. Yet they only made up about one-half of one percent of Syrian refugees admitted that year."[57]

We're glad that President Trump has committed to fixing this broken system and offering temporary shelter to those who really need it. Now it is time to hold wealthy, nearby Muslim countries responsible for looking out for their own.

We can help more refugees, facilitate an easier assimilation in a country with a similar cultural, language and religion, and make their return home a lot more efficient.

★ ★ ★

Elections Have Consequences

In October and November of 2016, the Obama administration admitted 18,300 "refugees" to the United States, overwhelmingly Muslims, from countries such as Syria, Iraq, and Somalia. In October and November of 2017, the Trump administration allowed in 3,108 refugees. The majority were Christians, with just 15 percent Muslims.[58]

Again, if someone can prove religious or ethnic persecution, let's grab 'em and give them shelter under the Bald Eagles' wings. Otherwise, for their sake as well as for ours, let's keep refugees closer to their home.

Also, to keep the number of new migrants and refugees manageable, we propose that for every refugee admitted, we reduce the immigration quota from that nation by one.

14. Enforce the financial promise made by sponsors to prevent immigrants from becoming a "public charge."

During the glory days of American immigration, those arriving at Ellis Island had to demonstrate and affirm they would not become a "public charge." This is a term used by U.S. immigration officials to refer to a person who is "likely to become primarily dependent on the government for subsistence, as demonstrated by either the receipt of public cash assistance for income maintenance or institutionalization for long-term care at government express."[59]

In other words, immigrants used to have to establish that they would not prove a financial burden to taxpayers—that they would not be feeding at the public trough. Their sponsors here would vow to assume all extra costs associated with the newcomer. Uncle Sam's pockets would not be picked.

Given just how much government assistance goes to immigrants, you may be surprised to learn this law is still on the books. Section 212(a) (4) of the Immigration and Nationality Act (INA), to be specific.[60]

We must hold sponsors to their promise to support the immigrant who is here in their name. (After all, that is what a sponsor is, right?)

This is not simply to benefit taxpaying Americans. It also benefits the immigrant. Building into future Americans a reliance on the government may help get Democrats elected. That's bad enough. Even worse, it absolutely destroys the motivation for self-sufficiency and self-determination that separates America from other nations. That has always been a motivation that turned an immigrant into a success story. How short-sighted of us to replace it with another cheap "entitlement."

Which gets to the last, but hardly least, piece of MISSION America.

15. Americanization

Finally, the capstone: doing everything we can to help immigrants become red-blooded flag-waving Americans.

If we want to Make America Great Again, one solid way is to Make Great Americans Again. Let's once again take those who come to our shores and make sure they appreciate, understand, and—dare we say it—*love* the United States of America. Let them learn our true history—not the distorted story of a people who robbed and pillaged and plundered (that wouldn't make us any different from any other country), but the tale of the first nation in history built on the principle that all men are created equal. A nation in which if you work hard you can rise above your station because you will be rewarded for your labors. Where you are responsible for yourself and those in your care, not a ward of anyone else, most especially not the government.

Americanization is the key to climbing the ladder of success. Those who don't want to accept it are really better off back home.

Though some of our suggestions may seem harsh measures aimed at those hoping to come to our country, make no mistake. The idea behind MISSION America is to create an engine of advancement not just for Americans but those who dream to be.

Without Americanization we don't have an America.

With it we have a stronger America in the years ahead, new flavors and all.

Give us ten thousand who come here with a heart that beats for the American Dream over ten enamored of radical politics or religion. Give us a hundred thousand immigrants who have seen tyranny and reject it over a hundred snowflakes who see a MAGA hat and cry "Nazi."

Those are the Great Americans in waiting.

Those are the ones who will become, as Hamilton said, a "harmony of ingredients."

It is they who can turn MISSION America into Mission Accomplished.

CHAPTER SEVEN

How to Sell Reality to People Allergic to Facts

The difficulty with rational solutions to our immigration crisis is that you have to try explaining them to irrational people. These folks are not just accidentally irrational—because they've had too much to drink, say, or just woke up. No, these people are selectively and programmatically irrational. Flouting the rules of fair argument to promote a favored cause makes them feel virtuous, as if it's evidence of just how committed to justice they really are.

Yes, we mean Progressives. They have one key advantage in any argument: they never have to worry about the logical implications of anything they say. Take them down their own road and after two steps they call you a racist or a something-or-other-phobe. Insist that you're just pointing how far down the slippery slope really goes, and they'll whip out one of their trusty "Get Out of Thought Free!" cards. They'll wave off the obvious implications of their premises, and roll their eyes at what a crackpot alarmist you are. Works every time. In the short run.

Those of us with long memories recall the late Phyllis Schlafly opposing the Equal Rights Amendment in part because it would lead to women in

Did you know?

★ Eighty percent of Central American women and girls who enter the United States illegally are raped along the way

★ Illegal immigration costs American taxpayers $116 billion a year

★ 147 million people from around world would like to move to the United States

combat and the end of single-sex restrooms. All the reasonable people har-rumphed that she was an extremist.

And wouldn't you know it, feminist logic gave us both of those things. But did Mrs. Schlafly get any credit for calling it, decades early? No. She was damned for tipping the enemy's hand, for *seeing those implications too soon*—before the public had been pummeled enough to be ready to accept them. That's what clear-thinking conservatives have to expect. Get used to it, and move on. (Mrs. Schlafly had the last laugh. Her last book, completed in the months before she died, made the conservative case for Donald Trump. He was elected not long after it appeared.)

The point of MISSION America is to strengthen the USA for future generations and secure its high ideals of liberty and equal opportunity (the Golden Egg) by keeping the country viable and cohesive (a live, healthy Goose). Even the resonant, controversial phrase "Putting America First" doesn't just mean placing America's interests before the UN's, the EU's, or MSNBC's. It also means that we must put America's future ahead of any discomfort we suffer from name-calling in the present. That is every good citizen's task—including yours.

To make it easier, here are some unsettling facts you should have at your fingertips. This list is ready for you to post on Facebook or Twitter, or bring up in conversation with lefty friends and relatives. (If you put these on social media, please do add a link to the Amazon page for this book, to help spread the word!)

Telling Facts to Answer the Progressives' "Idealism" and "Compassion"

- Eighty percent of Central American women and girls coming to the United States illegally are raped on the journey. That's an unavoidable outcome of our unsecured border, which lures the helpless and puts them at the mercy of the ruthless.[1]

- Taxpayers spend nearly $30 billion a year on non-emergency medical expenses for illegal immigrants. That's enough to buy health insurance for three million Americans.[2]

- States spend $44 billion a year to educate illegal immigrants. That's enough to build 1,660 new schools or hire more than 780,000 teachers.[3]

- The net cost of illegal immigrants to U.S. taxpayers is $116 billion a year. The gross cost is $135 billion, but they pay $19 billion in total taxes.[4]

- As we saw in chapter four, American wages have been flat or falling for decades—since not long after the 1965 beginning of the low-skill immigrant wave that has been crashing over our shores. What a weird, nutty coincidence...[5]

- Low-skill immigration hurts the poor. According to a 2015 Economic Policy Institute study, 37.4 percent of the working-age poor eligible for employment were not working. That includes the 3.3 million unemployed poor people that were seeking a job.[6]

- As we saw in chapter six, despite aliens, legal and illegal, being only 9 percent of the population, they make up 27 percent of all federal prisoners.[7]

- These prisoners have been arrested an average of eight times each, and charged with twelve crimes.[8]

- Unfettered Muslim immigration has turned Sweden from one of Europe's safest nations into one of its most dangerous. In response, Sweden stopped releasing data on the ethnicity of criminals in 2005 "because of the informal taboo on linking immigration to crime."[9]

- England and Wales saw a 27 percent jump in violent crime in 2015. A major factor? Growing violence among migrants, including organized gangs that target British girls for sexual exploitation.[10]

- Poland has refused EU pressure to take in Muslim migrants.[11] A State Department report on 2016 crime statistics notes that "Poland continues to be one of the safest countries in Europe."[12]

- The Islamic supremacist group Muslim Brotherhood created the front organization the Council on American-Islamic Relations (CAIR). That's the group which greets every Muslim terror attack with grave warnings about how Islamophobia is the real threat—not bombs, bullets, knives, or dedicated jihadists driving into helpless crowds of unarmed "infidels." The Brotherhood has been quite explicit on how it intends to extend the Islamic presence, then Islamic rule, throughout the West by a "Civilization-Jihadist Process…destroying the Western Civilization from within."[13]

- There is also a real, living breathing movement to reclaim a significant chunk of the United States for Mexico via "Reconquista." Its supporters point to the fact that several U.S. southwestern states did once belong to Mexico—which lost them in a war. Re-conquistadors want to claim them for Mexico today, one way or another. A leading advocate was Charles Trujillo of the University of New Mexico, who said that the "República del Norte" would be brought into existence by "any means necessary but that it was unlikely to be formed by civil war but rather by the electoral pressure of the future majority Hispanic population in the region." The next time you see illegal immigrants waving the flag of a country they are apparently desperate not to return to, remember that this may be what they have in mind. Be sure to ask them, and record their responses on your phone. Make memes and share them.[14]

- Forty percent of native-born Catholics leave the Church, and one in four U.S. Catholics is an immigrant.[15]
- Ninety-seven cents of every dollar the bishops spend on refugees is federal money, which props up top-heavy groups like Catholic Charities.[16]
- Globalist atheist mega-billionaire George Soros is buying pro-immigration church and para-church groups. His foundations promote same-sex marriage, abortion, and open borders.[17] Why do pastors take his money?
- Crime rates are higher among second- and third-generation immigrants, many of whom seem to be assimilating to the mores of America's underclass.[18]
- The fact that Mexico has a record-high murder rate—their drug wars have made our southern neighbor the second deadliest conflict zone in the world after Syria[19]—has become an argument *against* deporting illegal Mexican immigrants, even for declaring them "refugees."[20] That's how you get MS-13 in Baltimore.

Five Tips for Explaining Immigration Issues to the Open-Minded but Underinformed

1. **Start with facts**—like those above. Reassure them that your concerns about immigration arise from the real-world impacts of immigration, not some stupid prejudice.

2. **Make apt comparisons.** Point out that the reforms we suggest in this book would bring the United States more in line with

Canada and Australia, which give preferences to high-skill immigrants and limit the numbers.

3. **Remind them of our history.** Document the fact that vast waves of low-skill immigrants came only during one eighty-year period of American history—when the continent was mostly empty, we had endless manufacturing and farm job opportunities, and the welfare state didn't exist. Use some of those quotations from our Founders in chapter three.

4. **Note that elites personally benefit from the immigration status quo, which hurts ordinary Americans.** Remind the people to whom you're speaking that opinion makers and other elites who almost uniformly back high immigration *benefit from it economically*, and that they don't feel the sting of wage competition. If low-priced lawyers, reporters, congressional staffers, and pastors were flooding into the country, elites might be singing a different tune. You, on the other hand, are looking out for the little guy, and for the country as a whole.

5. **Accentuate the positive.** Try to smile and stay upbeat about your high hopes for our country. You want to give us a chance to harmonize all our ingredients, and encourage assimilation of immigrants—not keep all of them out forever.

Winsome Approaches to Try on the Initially Hostile or Worried

1. **Cite sensible statements by Democrats.** Point out that liberal Democratic icons such as Bill Clinton, Barbara Jordan, and Harry Reid all took strong stances against illegal immigration. Quote Jordan's stern recommendations on the issue

from chapter five. Were they all xenophobes? Or were they worried about our country's future?

2. **Answer anecdote with anecdote.** Everybody knows an inspiring story or two about a one-time illegal immigrant, or someone who came here with no apparent skills and made good. Respond with some of the anecdotes about terrorism and crime from chapter one. Then gently suggest that statistics are a better guide than individual instances.

3. **Praise law and order.** Ask the person to imagine all our streets without traffic lights or road signs, and our interstates without police. Remind him that this is the status quo on most of our country's southern border, which is controlled by narco-traffickers and human smugglers. Is it really godly or patriotic to shrug at systematic rape of migrant girls? At the exploitation of illegal workers in unsafe conditions where it's illegal for Americans to work? At the devaluing of U.S. citizenship to a prize in a lottery?

4. **Don't expect too much.** If you're contending with people who are genuine open-borders ideologues, you probably won't convince anyone at first. You might think you're making no impact at all. But don't give up. It could be that you're planting a seed of good sense that will sprout whenever it's watered. If you're debating on social media, remember that most of your audience consists of bystanders, not your opponent. Plenty of people will be hearing your arguments for the first time. You never know what good your words may be doing.

5. **Stay upbeat and hopeful.** It'll confuse the heck out of people who want to believe that you're a doomster or a hater. Always remember that you're not arguing *against immigrants* as people, but *for* our country, our system, and our future.

20 Questions You Can Ask in All Sincerity

1. Is all the "benefit" from illegal immigrants (cheap yard work, new taco trucks, more votes for Democrats) worth the life of one American killed by an illegal immigrant whom we didn't deport because of political correctness?

2. Was Alexander Hamilton wrong when he argued for a "harmony of ingredients" when considering who could immigrate?

3. Should an immigration policy be about creating diversity for diversity's sake? Punishing America for its past "sins"? Or strengthening America for the future?

4. Is it hypocritical to say that a wall is wrong when your own house has them?

5. Virtually every illegal immigrant who gets an amnesty, including Dreamers, will benefit from affirmative action preferences, compared to (say) white male combat veterans or displaced coal miners. Is that fair?

6. If you don't like our limits on legal immigration, exactly how many people do you want pouring into the country? What's the actual number?

7. One hundred forty-seven *million* people would like to move to the United States. Is it xenophobic to say "no" to any of them? If not, then to how many? Where do you draw the line?

8. The average immigrant in federal prison has been arrested eight times and charged with twelve crimes. How many crimes are you willing to accept before you're willing to kick them out of the country?

9. If illegals are doing the work Americans won't do, do you favor eliminating the minimum wage and safety regulations in those fields? Because that's what illegal immigration does, in effect.

10. Why would you be on the same side of this issue as George Soros, a bitter socialist with designs on reshaping the politics of dozens of countries via shadowy front groups?

11. Even if you want to take in "the huddled masses yearning to breathe free," don't you at least want to screen them for communicable diseases first?

12. How many more supporters of Sharia law does America need?

13. Would you rather your tax dollars go to an illegal immigrant or to help millions more Americans afford health insurance?

14. Would you rather your education tax dollars go to illegals or toward building new schools?

15. Even if you are fine with Dreamers staying in the United States, should they get to sponsor countless other immigrants—such as their parents, who snuck them in illegally?

16. What's wrong with an American immigration policy based on what's best for America?

17. Ronald Reagan famously said, "A nation that cannot control its borders is not a nation."[21] Where is he wrong and why?

18. Do you still believe in the American Dream? Do you think it was built on welfare programs and balkanized ethnic ghettos?

19. Isn't American immigration worth doing right, both for the immigrant and America?

20. How do you form newcomers into great Americans if you keep insisting that America isn't all that great, anyway?

Snappy Answers to Leftist One-Liners

America is a nation of immigrants!

Some of our ancestors weren't immigrants. They were slaves. Should we call America a nation of slaves? Or settlers and conquerors? They were in the mix too.

But immigration is what makes America unique.

No, it isn't. Argentina and Malaysia also took lots of immigrants. That's not what sets us apart. Liberty is.

Oh, you just want to keep America white!

Nonsense. I'd rather have a hundred thousand Filipino pro-life Republicans than five pro-choice, veal-pale social justice warriors. Now, I will cop to wanting to keep out future Democrats. But that's just being patriotic.

Immigrants add to the economy!

So why not 147 million? Why not one billion? Clearly there are costs as well as benefits, and we're arguing about the right balance. If you don't want to accept all comers, you're a restrictionist too. Welcome to the club.

Our diversity is our strength!

It wasn't for Yugoslavia, or Rwanda, or Northern Ireland. Sometimes it's a deep source of conflict that leads to bigger and bigger government and fewer freedoms. Look at how Western European countries are turning into police states to manage all their fresh new "diversity." There weren't always checkpoints on London Bridge, you know.

Immigrants give new entrepreneurial energy to lagging states.

Except when they impose so many costs and vote for so many leftist politicians that the natives flee for the hills. Or did millions of Californians decide that they just hated good weather and gorgeous beaches, so they'd rather live in Utah?

People are not illegal!

Nope. But their presence in our country is. If you find some squatter living in your basement, remember to call him an "undocumented tenant." Then pay for his medical care and his kids' college education.

They are "undocumented Americans!"

Ditto for your squatter. He's an "unofficial family member." Right? What's stupid about that slogan of yours is that it makes foreign citizens here illegally sound like kids who forgot their ID. In fact, a lot of them do have documents. They're just stolen from American victims of identity theft.

These are families you're trying to break up.

No. We're perfectly happy to send them all safely to their parents' home country, where they may legally reside. If they choose to break up their family by sneaking into the United States illegally, it's wrong for us to reward that. It's called "enabling."

You're Islamophobic!

A phobia is an irrational fear. When you have a significant percentage within a huge world religion who believe they are ordered by Allah to either convert, enslave, or kill you (not necessarily in that order), being on guard is highly rational. Also, that's a word invented by CAIR, a group founded by the terrorist Muslim Brotherhood to make radical Islam sound warm and fuzzy to Americans. How's it feel to be a terrorist propagandist?

Aren't you just a xenophobe?

Are you a xenomaniac?

We need sanctuary cities so that undocumented immigrants won't be afraid to cooperate with police to stop crime.

So you're saying we need to open our borders to populate our Neighborhood Watch programs?

Illegals are doing the work Americans don't want to do!

Not at illegal, semi-slave wages, they won't. What keeps those wages down, you think? Is it climate change, or a constant influx of low-skill off-the-books workers?

Immigrants have a work ethic that most Americans don't.

Some do. A lot of them end up on welfare, in a system they didn't pay into.

Illegal immigrants do not vote illegally in U.S. elections! That's a myth!

In the swing state of Pennsylvania alone, the government admits it has found hundreds of proven cases where they did. If this is such a non-problem, why do you object to requiring ID for voting—you know, like we require for driving?

You're a Christian. The Bible says to welcome the stranger.

Do you really think America should be governed by what the Bible says? Do you favor Bible study in public schools? No? Then why use it selectively to make our immigration laws?

What would Jesus do, huh, Christian guy?

Why don't you pray and ask him? He told us to "render unto Caesar what is Caesar's." That sure sounds like he respected the rule of law.

★ ★ ★

A Conversation You're Not Supposed to Have: The Last Religious Argument about Immigration That You'll Ever Need

Christian conservatives have fought for decades against the hijack of gospel compassion on the subject of immigration. We rarely lose on the arguments. That's not because we're geniuses. It's because our opponents hardly make any. They don't rebut our assertions, dispute our facts, or even address what we've said.

Instead of engaging logic, history, precedent, Church tradition, or even (for Catholics) the binding teaching of their own Church's Catechism, open-borders advocates tend to do something else. They strike elaborate postures that seem to them Christ-like. They weave emotional word pictures, play on emotions, and in general fuss and preen to attain one outcome: *they seem like better people.*

So even when champions of open borders don't make sense or get the facts wrong, too many Christians think that their statements are "coming from a good place." From a fuzzy, blurry, purple Jesusy kind of place. So open-borders fans lose the argument on points but win the battle for persuasion.

It's exhausting. It's like entering a fencing tournament and learning that your opponent is armed with a bowl of spaghetti. He gets points every time that sauce splatters your suit.

So let's change the rules.

Here's a model conversation between a defender of the classical Christian position on patriotism and sovereignty and a proponent of what we call "promiscuous citizenship." The speakers are named "Augustine" and "Pollyanna."

POLLYANNA: I hear that you've been going after immigrant-friendly Christians, because some of them accept financial support from a progressive foundation.

AUGUSTINE: You mean the foundation run by anti-Christian, anti-family, pro-abortion globalist socialist George Soros, the Open Society Project? Yes, I've been talking about that. I hope you do some research on it.

POLLYANNA: Well, of course as a Christian I don't believe all those other things. But at least he's trying to help people. Helpless, vulnerable, marginalized people. People like Jesus.

AUGUSTINE: How is it exactly that people leaving their native countries to go make more money somewhere else are like Jesus? Did He leave Israel to find better paying carpentry work in Athens?

POLLYANNA: No, but he was an illegal immigrant and a refugee. He crossed borders to flee oppression.

AUGUSTINE: Actually, his parents were more like fugitive members of a royal family. (They were both descended from King David.) When they heard that Herod was looking for Jesus, they temporarily moved from one province of the Roman empire to another. They crossed no international borders. They didn't break Roman law. They went to the "first safe country," Egypt, where Joseph worked for a living—legally. And then when it was safe, they went back home. So how exactly is that like Somalis flying over ten Muslim countries to go on welfare in the United States, attend Islamist mosques, and refuse to go home, ever?

POLLYANNA: You're just being legalistic now. Focusing in on details and missing the bigger picture.

AUGUSTINE: A picture is made up of details. Get them wrong, and you change the picture. So we've established that Jesus had little in common with beneficiaries of America's lavish, self-destructive refugee program. What else have you got?

POLLYANNA: Did you know that no American has ever died as a result of a terrorist attack by a refugee? I read that in *Christianity Today*.[22]

AUGUSTINE: What about the Boston Marathon bombers? They came here from Chechnya.

POLLYANNA: I looked that up on Snopes.com. And you're wrong. They weren't admitted under the Refugee Act, but the Asylum Act.

AUGUSTINE: I see. I'm sure that's a great comfort to the families of their victims. How about the Ohio State attack, where a Somali "refugee" admitted *under the correct Congressional statute* attacked American students with a machete? You know, to avenge the abuse of Muslims in...Burma.

POLLYANNA: None of those people died, did they?

AUGUSTINE: You're right. They are slowly recovering. So forget them. And we should also forget all the children of refugees who commit acts of terror in Europe. People whose parents were welcomed and supported by Western countries, where their kids drank in poison at Islamist madrasas. And we should forget their victims—except when we pause to celebrate how very diverse those victims are. The London police chief is mighty proud that the dead from a recent terrorist attack came from eight separate countries.[23]

POLLYANNA: Well, our diversity is our strength.

AUGUSTINE: So multiculturalism is a contest. *The country whose civilian corpses are the most diverse...wins.*

POLLYANNA: You are just so morbid and negative. That is not a gospel attitude.

AUGUSTINE: You mean the same gospel that warns us about eternal hellfire? That gospel? Or maybe you're thinking *Godspell*, the 1970s musical.

POLLYANNA: Again, you're just channeling some angry white male antipathy that you must have picked up from Donald Trump or Breitbart. Are you part of the Alt-Right?

AUGUSTINE: Quite the contrary. Alt-Right racists hate Christians. They think that Christianity is a civilizational suicide cult. I'm afraid that you do, too. It's just you want to embrace that act of self-annihilation. Jesus never preached suicide.

POLLYANNA: So now you speak for Jesus? Please...

AUGUSTINE: No, but I can quote him. He told the Pharisees "Render unto Caesar what is Caesar's," right?

POLLYANNA: Yes ...

AUGUSTINE: So let's try to see what is Caesar's, shall we? On the most literal level, it clearly includes minting coinage, and levying taxes, yes?

POLLYANNA: Right. Progressive taxes!

AUGUSTINE: What else would have to be Caesar's? What else belongs to the State and not the Church? Maybe controlling the police and army? You'd agree that the Church shouldn't have its own militias, wouldn't you?

POLLYANNA: No, of course not. That's like...the Inquisition.

AUGUSTINE: So what's another thing that Caesar and not the Church should control? Should the Church control our national borders and grant or withhold citizenship? If so, which Church? The Catholics? The Baptists?

POLLYANNA: No, obviously not.

AUGUSTINE: Okay, so then it's the State. The State controls the movement of peoples across our borders.

POLLYANNA: Yeah, but the Church can tell us that we need to welcome everyone. Then as Christians we have to honor that.

AUGUSTINE: And impose it on our fellow citizens, who aren't even Christians? Why not impose the whole Bible on them, then? Why not force them to convert?

POLLYANNA: Because that violates the separation of Church and State.

AUGUSTINE: And the Church setting immigration policy based not on reason, prudence, the common good, or the natural law—but on our readings of the gospel? That's not a problem? Should the Church censor movies too? Maybe run all our state universities?

POLLYANNA: But this is different. You know a lot of those immigrants you want to turn away are Christians. Most are Catholics just like you.

AUGUSTINE: So I should bias my opinion about what's best for my fellow citizens to benefit strangers from another country because they belong to my Church? I should try to fill up the emptying pews of my denomination, because our leaders can't catechize or evangelize?

POLLYANNA: I just think you should "welcome the stranger." It says that in Exodus 22:21, and that is unconditional.

AUGUSTINE: Three verses earlier, in Exodus 22:18, the Bible demands the death penalty for witches. No exceptions. Should we implement that, too? Or maybe we shouldn't cherry-pick the Old Testament for proof-texts to impose on our fellow citizens. How about that?

POLLYANNA: I believe in the absolute embrace of the Other. That's what the gospel means to me.

AUGUSTINE: Okay. But you know that virtually no Christians have ever believed that, right? Many of the first Christians to emerge from the catacombs after Constantine joined the Roman army to fight the barbarians. The saint I'm named for, Augustine, prayed that Rome could stop those armies of immigrants from entering the empire. Because he thought they were bad for the common good.

POLLYANNA: Well, plenty of Christians have perverted the gospel over the centuries.

AUGUSTINE: Did every Christian country in history up until the 1980s or so? Are your generation of believers the best Christians in history?

POLLYANNA: I don't make any great claims. But on this, I know I stand with the immigrant.

AUGUSTINE: How many of them will you stand with? All of them?

POLLYANNA: Yes. It's a principled stand.

AUGUSTINE: According to the Gallup Poll, "Nearly 710 million adults worldwide want to migrate to another country and 147 million of those specifically want to come to the United States."[24]

POLLYANNA: Wow. Okay.

AUGUSTINE: So do you favor allowing all 147 million of those people to come to the United States, and receive the same social support as citizens?

POLLYANNA: Well, that's a little extreme.

AUGUSTINE: Ah, so you do favor immigration restriction.

POLLYANNA: I mean, there have to be limits of some kind.

AUGUSTINE: Finally! We agree. You and I both think that the government has the right to say "no" to immigrants. We're just arguing over how many we should accept, and under what conditions. Right?

POLLYANNA: Er, okay.

AUGUSTINE: Or you could take all 147 million. Regardless of their effect on the American poor, on the environment, on jobs and wages, and civic order—because a lot of them will want to impose Sharia, you know. A lot of them. So you want to take all of them?

POLLYANNA: Okay, no.

AUGUSTINE: Great! We're on the same side. I'm glad we could reason together. Now, why don't you come with me. I could use some help building a wall . . .

A Letter to Our Grandparents

Dearest Grandpa and Grandma Zmirak, Williams, Perrotta, and Pellegrino,

We cannot end this journey without one more thanks for *your* journey. You boarded the boats and left behind the life you knew, for a new land, a new Constitution.

What did you feel when you first spotted Lady Liberty from the harbor? Or took your first step on American soil. Awe? Fear? Excitement? Trepidation? Gratitude?

What we do know is that in short order you got to *work*. You sweated and struggled and became Americans. Because of you, your children, grandchildren, great-grandchildren and now great-great-grandchildren have all been proud Americans.

Look at us: When you stepped on Ellis Island did you anticipate a grandson who'd get to go to Yale and write articles that get attacked by liberals in the Vatican? Probably not. Did you imagine a grandson who'd make a living making people laugh? No, but you'd probably say, "Only in America."

Now the son of a Croatian-American postal worker from Hell's Kitchen and the son of an Italian-American musician from Jersey are working together in Texas, writing a book on a major national issue for one of the top publishers in America—and hashing out that book at Mexican, Italian, and Indian restaurants. "Only in America."

That phrase "Only in America" has endless resonance. There have been countless political entities over the millennia of human history—kingdoms, principalities, empires, and utopian ideological projects. None of them achieved what America has, crafting "out of many, one." In freedom, with opportunities (eventually) for all.

It's that secret ingredient, "Only in America," that led millions from every corner of God's green earth to forsake all and sail the sea for our shores.

Neil Diamond—the Jewish descendent of Russian and Polish immigrants—brought the point home in his anthem "America."

Everywhere around the world, they're coming to America.
Got a dream to take them there, they're coming to America

The bridge borrows from one of our patriotic hymns:

My country, 'tis of thee, sweet land of liberty,
Of thee I sing.

Those are lyrics your children learned in school, maybe sang for you at home. You didn't resent that and insist that they wall themselves off from their new country's songs and stories. With a twinge of wistfulness about all the good things back in the Old Country, you welcomed it. You were proud to bring up young... *Americans.* The chances that this land would offer them, would offer us, were music to your ears.

You would be disheartened to know that many who come to our shores no longer sing of this sweet land of liberty. They shout against a land of oppression, unjust suffering, and victimization. Some even plot against it.

Unlike you, who traveled here from lands of real poverty and tyranny, they're utterly ungrateful for America's unexampled prosperity and freedom. That's why we, your grandchildren, needed to write this book. What you embraced, we defend. That's a tribute to you.

Over and over again we have returned to Hamilton's notion of a "harmony of ingredients." Diversity for diversity's sake, amplified divisions, yields nothing but painful dissonance. It's noise and confusion, not harmony. And it's damaging. The four of you would hold your ears if you heard what's playing now.

Your legacy merits better. So do today's Americans. And those hoping to become Americans in the future. That's why the conductor (our Constitutional government) needs to wave the baton and call the orchestra to order. To tune up and play together.

What we've tried to do with this book is honor you, to apply wisdom and compassion to an issue that has sown much folly and division in our day. We're not trying to recreate the past, but to build for the future. We know that around the world—whether it be in a mountain hamlet in Italy, a village in Ireland, a port in the Adriatic, or a thirsty village in Ethiopia—there are those who hear the song of freedom, who wish to swell the music. But that can't happen if we let the melody die and be forgotten. We must preserve and pass it on.

One song, one nation, under God, indivisible, with liberty and justice for all.

Sincerely,

John and Al

Acknowledgments

I would like to thank James Robison and all the staff at Life Outreach International, and Jay Richards in particular. My thanks to Faye Ballard, and all those who have supported my aspirations to write on this crucial subject over many years. And many thanks to Finnegan and Rayne Zmirak, without whose canine interventions this book would have been finished months sooner.

—John Zmirak

I'd like to thank the letter J for making my role in this project possible:

John Zmirak. Thank you for entrusting me to help you make this book happen. Your welcoming heart and generous creative spirit—and taste in restaurants—made doing this a joy. Being a coauthor with you is a treat. Being a friend and colleague is an honor.

James Robison. Without your vision of an ecumenical site fixed on drawing together streams of wisdom, the Catholic Harvard grad from New York and the Charismatic comedy writer from Maryland would never have met. I am also so grateful for the passion and support and encouragement and inspiration you have shown me and all of the rest of us at The Stream.

Jesus Christ. Yes, you are my Lord and Savior. But the tiny miracles you weaved together to make this particular book happen fill me with awe and could fill another book. Truly you order my steps.

I'd also like to acknowledge the fine folks at Regnery: Elizabeth, Tom, Gary, and the rest for their kindness and believing I could be of service on this project. I look forward to working with you all again.

—Al Perrotta

Notes

Introduction

1. Charles Camosy, "Bishop Says Deporting Migrants 'Not Unlike' Abortion," Crux, July 26, 2016, https://cruxnow.com/interviews/2016/07/26/camosy-interview-bp-brownsville-tx/.
2. Russell Moore, "Immigration and the Gospel," Russell Moore, June 17, 2011, https://www.russellmoore.com/2011/06/17/immigration-and-the-gospel/.
3. Pascal-Emmanuel Gobry, "I Am Catholic—and I Don't Know What I'm Supposed to Believe about Immigration," *America*, September 12, 2017, https://www.americamagazine.org/politics-society/2017/09/12/i-am-catholic-and-i-dont-know-what-im-supposed-believe-about.
4. Catechism of the Catholic Church, 2241, http://www.scborromeo.org/ccc/para/2241.htm.
5. Gobry, "I Am Catholic."
6. Neli Esipova and Julie Ray, "700 Million Worldwide Desire to Migrate Permanently," Gallup News, November 2, 2009, http://news.gallup.com/poll/124028/700-million-worldwide-desire-migrate-permanently.aspx

Chapter One: Houston, We've Got a Problem

1. Tim Hains, "'Latino Victory Fund' Ad Depicts Ed Gillespie Supporter Terrorizing Minority Children," Real Clear Politics, October 30, 2017, https://www.realclearpolitics.com/video/2017/10/30/latino_victory_fund_ad_depicts_ed_gillespie_supporter_terrorizing_minority_children.html.
2. Tina Moore, Larry Celona, and Danika Fears, "8 Killed as Truck Plows into Pedestrians in Downtown NYC Terror Attack," *New York Post,* October 31, 2017, http://nypost.com/2017/10/31/8-killed-truck-pedestrians-downtown-nyc-terror-attack/.

3. "Why Europe Needs More Migrants," *Economist*, July 12, 2017, https://www.economist.com/blogs/graphicdetail/2017/07/daily-chart-6.

4. To address this problem without enforcing our country's immigration laws, states such as California are trying (without much success) to convince illegal immigrants to buy auto insurance. Josie Huang, "Calif. to Offer Low-Cost Insurance to New Immigrant Drivers," KPCC, December 31, 2014, http://www.scpr.org/blogs/multiamerican/2014/12/31/17743/calif-low-cost-insurance-immigrant-drivers/.

5. "Identity and Immigration Status of 9/11 Terrorists," Federation for American Immigration Reform, January 2011, https://fairus.org/issue/national-security/identity-and-immigration-status-911-terrorists.

6. Riley Walters, "Islamist Terrorist Attacks and Plots Against the US Homeland Rise to 92," The Daily Signal, October 20, 2016, http://dailysignal.com/2016/10/20/islamist-terrorist-attacks-and-plots-against-the-u-s-homeland-rise-to-92/.

7. Laura Pitel and Arthur Beesley, "Erdogan Threatens to Let 3m Refugees into Europe," *Financial Times*, November 25, 2016, https://www.ft.com/content/c5197e60-b2fc-11e6-9c37-5787335499a0.

8. Austin York, "OSU Attacker Came to America by Way of Dallas," CBS DFW, November 28, 2016, http://dfw.cbslocal.com/2016/11/28/osu-attacker-came-to-america-by-way-of-dallas/.

9. Ann Corcoran, "In 2014, Your Tax Dollars Paid 97% of the US Conference of Catholic Bishops Migration Fund Budget," Refugee Resettlement Watch, July 25, 2015, https://refugeeresettlementwatch.wordpress.com/2015/07/25/in-2014-your-tax-dollars-paid-97-of-the-us-conference-of-catholic-bishops-migration-fund-budget/.

10. 2014 IRS Form 990 for Catholic Charities of Dallas, GuideStar, http://www.guidestar.org/FinDocuments/2015/752/745/2015-752745221-0c652f22-9.pdf.

11. "Why the bishop of Dallas sheltered a family on Ebola watch," CNA/EWTN News, Oct 21, 2014, http://www.catholicnewsagency.com/news/why-the-bishop-of-dallas-sheltered-a-family-on-ebola-watch-83075/.

12. Jim Stinson, "Somali Refugee Resettlement Up 250 Percent under Obama," Lifezette, November 29, 2016, http://www.lifezette.com/polizette/somali-refugees-290-percent-obama/?utm_content=buffere7fca&utm_medium=social&utm_source=twitter.com&utm_campaign=buffer.

13. See "What is Wahabism? The Reactionary Branch of Islam from Saudi Arabia Said to Be 'the Main Source of Global Terrorism," *Daily Telegraph*, May 19, 2017, http://www.telegraph.co.uk/news/2016/03/29/what-is-wahhabism-the-reactionary-branch-of-islam-said-to-be-the/.

14. "Refugee Status under International Law," European Parliamentary Research Service Blog, October 27, 2015, https://epthinktank.eu/2015/10/27/refugee-status-under-international-law/.

15. Faith McDonnell, "Scandal: U.S. Christian Groups Prioritize Muslim Refugees over Christian Ones. Here's Why," The Stream, November 16, 2015, https://stream.org/us-christian-groups-prioritizing-muslim-over-christian/.

16. Jack Montgomery, "French Presidential Favourite Macron: Terrorism 'Part of Our Daily Lives for Years to Come' After Paris Shooting," Breitbart, April 21, 2017, http://www.breitbart.com/london/2017/04/21/macron-terrorism-part-daily-lives-years-paris-shooting/.

17. Neil Munro, "Courts Block DHS Review of Refugee Threats," Breitbart, May 10, 2017, http://www.breitbart.com/big-government/2017/05/10/courts-block-dhs-review-refugee-threats/.

18. Elizabeth Roberts, "Report: Mexico Was Second Deadliest Country in 2016," CNN, May 10, 2017, http://www.cnn.com/2017/05/09/americas/mexico-second-deadliest-conflict-2016/index.html.

19. Kimberley Amadeo, "How the 9/11 Attacks Still Affect the Economy Today," The Balance, January 17, 2017, https://www.thebalance.com/how-the-9-11-attacks-still-affect-the-economy-today-3305536.

20. Edward C. Banfield, The Moral Basis of a Backward Society (Glencoe, IL: The Free Press: 1967); Stanley Kurtz, "I and My Brother against my Cousin," Ethics and Public Policy Center, n.d., https://eppc.org/publications/i-and-my-brother-against-my-cousin/.

21. Justin Caruso, "6.8 MILLION: How Birthright Citizenship Is Changing US Elections," The Daily Caller News Foundation, November 5, 2016, http://dailycaller.com/2016/11/05/6-8-million-how-birthright-citizenship-is-changing-u-s-elections/.

22. "About the Center for Immigration Studies," The Center for Immigration Studies, https://cis.org/About-Center-Immigration-Studies.

23. "Extremist Files," Southern Poverty Law Center, Extremist Files, https://www.splcenter.org/fighting-hate/extremist-files/groups?keyword=center+for+immigration.

24. "Italian Immigration," Digital History, 2016, http://www.digitalhistory.uh.edu/voices/italian_immigration.cfm.

25. Stephen A. Camarota, "Welfare Use by Immigrant and Native Households," Center for Immigration Studies, September 2015, http://cis.org/Welfare-Use-Immigrant-Native-Households.

26. Ibid.

27. Jason Richwine, "The Cost of Welfare Use by Immigrant and Native Households," Center for Immigration Studies, May 9, 2016, https://cis.org/Report/Cost-Welfare-Use-Immigrant-and-Native-Households.

28. Steven A. Camarota, "The Cost of a Border Wall vs. the Cost of Illegal Immigration," February 15, 2017, https://cis.org/Report/Cost-Border-Wall-vs-Cost-Illegal-Immigration.

29. Amanda Ulrich, "Women Say Muslim-Majority Areas in French Suburbs Are Now NO-GO Areas for Females Where They Are Banned from Mixing with Men and Must Dress Conservatively," Daily Mail, December 14, 2016, http://www.dailymail.co.uk/news/article-4032680/Undercover-footage-reveals-no-zones-women-France-s-majority-Muslim-suburbs.html.

30. Peter Skerry, "Do We Really Want Immigrants to Assimilate?" The Brookings Institution, March 1, 2000, https://www.brookings.edu/articles/do-we-really-want-immigrants-to-assimilate/.

31. Heather Mac Donald, "The Immigrant Gang Plague," City Journal, Summer 2004, https://www.city-journal.org/html/immigrant-gang-plague-12801.html.

32. Heather Mac Donald, "California's Demographic Revolution," City Journal, Winter 2012, https://www.city-journal.org/html/california%E2%80%99s-demographic-revolution-13440.html; See also Rich Morin, "Crime rises among second-generation

immigrants as they assimilate," Pew Research, October 15, 2013, http://www.pewresearch.org/fact-tank/2013/10/15/crime-rises-among-second-generation-immigrants-as-they-assimilate/.

33.   American Patrol newsletter, October 1996, http://www.americanpatrol.com/RECONQUISTA/AZTLAN.html.

34.   "Will California's Leftist K-12 Curriculum Go National?" Stanley Kurtz, *National Review*, June 1, 2016, http://www.nationalreview.com/corner/436083/will-californias-leftist-k-12-curriculum-go-national.

35.   George Borjas, "Yes, Immigration Hurts American Workers," Politico, September/October 2016, http://www.politico.com/magazine/story/2016/09/trump-clinton-immigration-economy-unemployment-jobs-214216.

36.   Rachel Stoltfoos, "Harvard Economist: Immigration Costs US Workers $500 Billion A Year," The Daily Caller News Foundation, March 16, 2016, http://dailycaller.com/2016/03/16/harvard-economist-immigration-costs-us-workers-500-billion-a-year-video/.

37.   Andrew C. McCarthy, "Investigate Racism in the Obama Justice Department," *National Review*, September 28, 2010, http://www.nationalreview.com/article/247956/investigate-racism-obama-justice-department-andrew-c-mccarthy.

Chapter Two: The History of Immigration in America

1.   See the aforementioned *Inventing Freedom* by Daniel Hannan (New York: Broadside Books, 2013) for an eloquent explanation of the unique heritage of ordered liberty that arose in England and spread through the "Anglosphere," but, sadly, to almost no place else.

2.   "History of Laws Concerning Immigration and Naturalization in the United States," Wikipedia, https://en.wikipedia.org/wiki/History_of_laws_concerning_immigration_and_naturalization_in_the_United_States.

3.   Catherine Rampbell, "Founding Fathers, Trashing Immigration," *Washington Post*, August 28, 2015, https://www.washingtonpost.com/news/rampage/wp/2015/08/28/founding-fathers-trashing-immigrants/?utm_term=.3b867e1a1e3a.

4.   Ben Franklin, "Letter to Peter Collinson," May 9, 1953, http://teachingamericanhistory.org/library/document/letter-to-peter-collinson/.

5.   Ibid.

6.   Ibid.

7.   Ibid.

8.   Michelle Malkin, "Immigration and the Values of the Founders," *National Review*, December 11, 2015, http://www.nationalreview.com/article/428359/immigration-founding-fathers-view-michelle-malkin.

9.   George Washington, AZ Quotes, http://www.azquotes.com/quote/540936.

10.   George Washington, AZ Quotes, http://www.azquotes.com/quote/1361507.

11.   George Washington, AZ Quotes, http://www.azquotes.com/quote/540918.

12.   Jerome Hudson, "Tolerance: 'Hamilton' Cast Lectures Mike Pence from Broadway Stage," Breitbart, November 19, 2016, http://www.breitbart.com/big-hollywood/2016/11/19/tolerance-hamilton-cast-lectures-mike-pence-broadway-stage/.

13.   Malkin, "Immigration and the Values of Our Founders."

14. Frank Fluckiger, "Tell the Truth about Immigration: The Founding Fathers Did," The American Constitutionist, vol. 4, issue 8, October 2015, http://www.constitutionparty.com/assets/2015.09-American-Constitutionist-September.pdf.

15. For instance, in 1806, when (later saint) Elizabeth Anne Seton converted to Catholicism, members of the New York Legislature debated expelling her from the state to stop her from proselytizing. See Derek Rotty, "Mother Seton: Servant of the Good Teacher," *Crisis*, January 2, 2014, http://www.crisismagazine.com/2014/mother-seton-servant-of-the-good-teacher.

16. John Simpkin, "Immigration to the USA: 1820–1860," Spartacus Educational, http://spartacus-educational.com/USAE1820.htm.

17. David Hackett Fischer, *Albion's Seed: Four British Folkways in America* (Oxford University Press, 1989).

18. Jay P. Dolan, *The Irish Americans: A History* (Bloomsbury Press, 2010), 67–83.

19. Lorraine Boissoneualut, "How the 19th-Century Know Nothing Party Reshaped American Politics," Smithsonian, January 26, 2017, https://www.smithsonianmag.com/history/immigrants-conspiracies-and-secret-society-launched-american-nativism-180961915/.

20. Clay Coppedge, "A Short History of Beer in Texas," TexasEscapes, http://www.texasescapes.com/ClayCoppedge/Short-history-of-beer-in-Texas.htm.

21. Boissoneualut, "How the 19th-Century Know Nothing Party."

22. Ibid.

23. "Memory and Reconciliation: The Church and the Faults of the Past," December 1999, http://www.vatican.va/roman_curia/congregations/cfaith/cti_documents/rc_con_cfaith_doc_20000307_memory-reconc-itc_en.html.

24. Leo XIII, "Testem Benevolentiae Nostrae", January 22, 1899, http://www.papalencyclicals.net/leo13/l13teste.htm.

25. William Stern, "How Dagger John Saved New York's Irish," *City Journal*, Spring 1997.

26. John Zmirak, *The Bad Catholic's Guide to Wine, Whiskey & Song: A Spirited Look at Catholic Life & Lore from the Apocalypse to Zinfandel* (New York: The Crossroad Publishing Company, 2007).

27. Geoffrey Ward, *The West: An Illustrated History* (Little, Brown & Co., 1997), 147.

28. Tim Yang, "The Malleable yet Undying Nature of the Yellow Peril," Dartmouth College, February 19, 2004), http://www.dartmouth.edu/~hist32/History/S22%20-The%20Malleable%20Yet%20Undying%20Nature%20of%20the%20Yellow%20Peril.htm.

29. "The Chinese and the Exclusion Act" *The North American Review*, University of Northern Iowa. 173:541 (December 1901): 782–789. JSTOR 25105257.

30. "Coolies," ImmigrationtoUnitedStates.org, http://immigrationtounitedstates.org/449-coolies.html.

31. "The People's Vote: 100 Documents that Shaped America," *U.S News & World Report*, 2003, https://web.archive.org/web/20070328223654/http://www.usnews.com/usnews/documents/docpages/document_page47.htm, excerpted from Teaching with Documents: Using Primary Sources From the National Archives (Washington, DC: National Archives and Records Administration, 1989), 82–85.

32. Gabriel J. Chin "Segregation's Last Stronghold: Race Discrimination and the Constitutional Law of Immigration," UCLA Law Review, 46:1 (1998). SSRN 1121119.

33. R. J. Rummel, "Power Kills: Genocide and Mass Murder," University of Hawaii, https://hawaii.edu/powerkills/POWER.ART.HTM.

34. Judy Chu, press release, "House Passes Rep. Judy Chu's Resolution of Regret for the Chinese Exclusion Act," June 19, 2012, https://chu.house.gov/press-release/house-passes-rep-judy-chu%E2%80%99s-resolution-regret-chinese-exclusion-act.

35. "Questions Asked of Immigrants at Ellis Island," North Texas Institute for Education, https://ntieva.unt.edu/pages/about/newsletters/vol_11/issue1/questions.htm

36. "Arrival at the Island and Initial Inspection," Statue of Liberty–Ellis Island Foundation, https://www.libertyellisfoundation.org/ellis-island-history#Arrival.

37. Whyatt Kingseed, "President McKinley Assassinated by an Anarchist," HistoryNet, October 1, 2001, http://www.historynet.com/president-william-mckinley-assassinated-by-an-anarchist.htm. Apparently Thomas Edison filmed the execution to educate people on the dangers of direct current. (His company provided alternating current.) You can see the film of Czolgosz's execution on the Internet. Thenightmarezone, "Electricution [sic] of Leon Czolgosz" Youtube, October 6, 2006, https://www.youtube.com/watch?v=UYSxfyIqrjs.

38. James Barrett, *The Irish Way: Becoming American in the Multiethnic City.* (Penguin, New York: 2012), 1–12.

39. John F. McClymer, *War and Welfare: Social Engineering in America, 1890–1925*, (1980) 79, 105–52

40. *The Home Teacher: The Act, with a Working Plan and Forty Lessons in English* (The Commission of Immigration and Housing in California, 1915).

41. "Eugenicists Dread Tainted Aliens," *New York Times*, September 25, 1921. http://query.nytimes.com/gst/abstract.html?res=9803E2DB123EEE3ABC4D51DFBF66838A639EDE&legacy=true.

42. Paul Rahe, "Woodrow Wilson: This So-Called Progressive was a Dedicated Racist," FEE.org,https://fee.org/articles/woodrow-wilson-progressive-and-dedicated-racist/.

43. Woodrow Wilson, "Third Annual Message to Congress", December 7, 1915. http://www.presidency.ucsb.edu/ws/print.php?pid=29556.

44. David D. Cole, "Enemy Aliens," *Stanford Law Review* 54:5 (2003): 953–1004. JSTOR 1229690. OCLC 95029839. doi:10.2307/1229690. Archived from the original (PDF) on May 3, 2011.

45. 1921 Emergency Quota Law, U.S. Immigration Legislation Online, http://library.uwb.edu/Static/USimmigration/1921_emergency_quota_law.html.

46. The Immigration Act of 1924 (The Johnson-Reed Act), Office of the Historian, Department of State, https://history.state.gov/milestones/1921-1936/immigration-act.

47. Ibid.

48. Robert K. Murray, *The 103rd Ballot: Democrats and the Disaster in Madison Square Garden* (New York: Harper & Row, 1976), 7.

49. Steven G. Koven and Frank Götzke, *American Immigration Policy: Confronting the Nation's Challenges* (New York: Springer, 2010), 133.

50. "U.S. Immigration After 1965," History, http://www.history.com/topics/us-immigration-since-1965.

51. Sen. Ted Kennedy, U.S. Senate, Subcommittee on Immigration and Naturalization of the Committee on the Judiciary, Washington, DC, February 10, 1965, 1–3; and quoted by Katie McHugh, "Ted Kennedy's Real Legacy: 50 Years of Ruinous Immigration

Law," Breitbart, March 30, 2015, http://www.breitbart.com/big-government/2015/03/30/ted-kennedys-real-legacy-50-years-of-ruinous-immigration-law/.

52. "U.S. Immigration After 1965," History, http://www.history.com/topics/us-immigration-since-1965.

53. Ibid.

54. Caroline May, "Total Net Employment Gains in the U.S.—Since the Recession—Still Went to the Foreign Born," Breitbart, March 6, 2015, http://www.breitbart.com/big-government/2015/03/06/total-net-employment-gains-in-the-u-s-since-the-recession-still-went-to-foreign-born/.

55. "US Immigration Legislation Online," University of Washington Bothell Library, http://library.uwb.edu/Static/USimmigration/USimmigrationlegislation.html.

56. "End Chain Migration," Numbers USA, https://www.numbersusa.com/solutions/end-chain-migration

57. Spencer Raley, "What Is Chain Migration?" Federation for American Immigration Reform, November 9, 2017, https://fairus.org/issue/legal-immigration/chain-migration.

58. Brendan Kirby, "Americans Overwhelmingly Favor End to Chain Migration, Poll Says," Lifezette, January 3, 2018, https://www.lifezette.com/polizette/americans-overwhelmingly-favor-end-to-chain-migration-poll-says/.

59. Alan Feuer, "Suspect in Times Square Bombing Leaves Trail of Mystery," *New York Times*, December 11, 2017, https://www.nytimes.com/2017/12/11/nyregion/akayed-ullah-port-authority-bombing-suspect.html; Sarah Maslin Nir and William K. Rashbaum, "Bomber Strikes near Times Square, Disrupting City but Killing None," *New York Times*, December 11, 2017, https://www.nytimes.com/2017/12/11/nyregion/explosion-times-square.html.

60. FAIR website, https://fairus.org/; "About FAIR," FAIR website, https://fairus.org/about-fair.

61. Jason DeParle, "The Anti-Immigration Crusader," *New York Times*, April 17, 2011.

62. Fred Dews, "What Percentage of U.S. Population is Foreign Born?" Brookings Institute, October 3, 2013, https://www.brookings.edu/blog/brookings-now/2013/10/03/what-percentage-of-u-s-population-is-foreign-born/.

Chapter Three: What Is America, Anyway?

1. John Sides, "What Makes Someone a 'Real' American? 93% of Americans Actually Agree on This." *Washington Post*, July 14, 2017, https://www.washingtonpost.com/news/monkey-cage/wp/2017/07/14/whats-very-important-to-being-american-93-of-americans-actually-agree-on-this/?utm_term=.42ec38265294.

2. Dinesh D'Souza, "Why Barack Obama is an Anti-Colonialist," *Washington Post*, October 8, 2010, http://www.washingtonpost.com/wp-dyn/content/article/2010/10/07/AR2010100705485.html.

3. Brian Ross and Rehab El-Buri, "Obama's Pastor: God Damn America, US to Blame for 9/11," ABC News, March 13, 2008. http://abcnews.go.com/Blotter/DemocraticDebate/story?id=4443788&page=1.

4. James Green, "Howard Zinn's History," *The Chronicle of Higher Education*, May 23, 2003, https://www.howardzinn.org/zinns-history-chronicle-of-higher-ed/.

5. Cliff Kincaide, "Leftist 'Historian' Howard Zinn Lied About Red Ties," Accuracy in Media, July 20, 2010, http://www.aim.org/aim-column/leftist-%E2%80%9Chistorian%E2%80%9D-howard-zinn-lied-about-red-ties/.

6. Michael Kazin, "Howard Zinn's History Lessons," *Dissent*, Spring 2004, https://www.dissentmagazine.org/article/howard-zinns-history-lessons.

7. Paul Seton, "The Papal View from the Global South," *First Things*, April 20, 2017, https://www.firstthings.com/web-exclusives/2017/04/the-papal-view-from-the-global-south.

8. "The Goose & the Golden Egg" in *The Aesop for Children*, Library of Congress, http://read.gov/aesop/091.html.

9. John Zmirak, "America the Abstraction," *The American Conservative*, January 13, 2003, http://www.theamericanconservative.com/articles/america-the-abstraction/.

10. Ramesh Ponnuru and Rich Lowry, "For Love of Country," *National Review*, February 20, 2017, https://www.nationalreview.com/magazine/2017-02-20-0000/donald-trump-inauguration-speech-and-nationalism.

11. Jonah Goldberg, "The Trouble with Nationalism," *National Review*, February 7, 2017, http://www.nationalreview.com/article/444694/nationalism-patriotism-donald-trump-response-national-review-cover-story.

12. Ben Shapiro, "Trump Has Brought European-Style Nationalism to the U.S.," February 8, 2017, http://www.nationalreview.com/article/444687/donald-trump-nationalism-should-worry-conservatives.

13. "Rep. Gutiérrez on Paul Ryan and Immigration" (press release), United States Congressman Luis V. Gutiérrez, October 23, 2015, https://gutierrez.house.gov/press-release/rep-guti%C3%A9rrez-paul-ryan-and-immigration.

14. Erica Werner, "Speaker Ryan to House GOP: Trump Proposal 'Not Who We Are,'" Associated Press, December 8, 2015, http://www.apnewsarchive.com/2015/Speaker-Ryan-to-House-GOP-Trump-comments-on-Muslims-not-who-we-are-violates-Constitution/id-31101077e0984012828da7562c76e771.

15. Avi Issacharoff, "450 of 452 Suicide Attacks in 2015 Were by Muslim Extremists, Study Shows," Times of Israel, January 8, 2016, https://www.timesofisrael.com/450-of-452-suicide-attacks-in-2015-were-by-muslim-extremists-study-shows/.

16. "The Immigration and Nationality Act of 1952 (The McCarran-Walter Act)," Office of the Historian, U.S. Department of State, https://history.state.gov/milestones/1945-1952/immigration-act.

17. Warner MacKenzie, "Understanding *Taqiyya* Islamic Principle of Lying for the Sake of Allah," Islam Watch, April 30, 2007, http://www.islam-watch.org/Warner/Taqiyya-Islamic-Principle-Lying-for-Allah.htm.

Chapter Four: Who Backs Our Unsustainable Status Quo?

1. Byron York, "Study Finds More Immigrants Equals More Democrats and More Losses for GOP," *Washington Examiner*, April 15, 2014, http://www.washingtonexaminer.com/study-finds-more-immigrants-equals-more-democrats-and-more-losses-for-gop/article/2547220.

2. Arian Campo Flores, "Pushing Obama on Immigration Reform," *Newsweek*, November 29, 2010, http://www.newsweek.com/pushing-obama-immigration-reform-70093.

Notes

3. James Gimple, "Immigration's Impact on Republican Political Prospects, 1980 to 2012," Center for Immigration Studies, April 15, 2014, https://cis.org/Immigrations-Impact-Republican-Political-Prospects-1980-2012.

4. "Maryland City Rescinds Vote that Allowed Illegal Immigrants to Ballot in Local Elections," Fox News, September 16, 2017, http://www.foxnews.com/politics/2017/09/16/maryland-city-rescinds-vote-that-allowed-illegal-immigrants-to-ballot-in-local-elections.html.

5. Andrew Sullivan, "The Issue That Could Lose the Next Election for Democrats," October 20, 2017, *New York*, http://nymag.com/daily/intelligencer/2017/10/the-issue-that-could-lose-the-next-election-for-democrats.html.

6. Peter Beinart, "How the Democrats Lost Their Way on Immigration," *Atlantic*, July/August 2017, https://www.theatlantic.com/magazine/archive/2017/07/the-democrats-immigration-mistake/528678/.

7. My-Thuan Tran, "Rival Denounces Rep. Sanchez's Comments About Vietnamese," *Los Angeles Times*, September 25, 2010, http://articles.latimes.com/2010/sep/25/local/la-me-0925-sanchez-vietnamese-20100925.

8. Henry Olsen, "The Democrats' Stance on Immigration Can Lead to Electoral Disaster," *Los Angeles Times*, March 16, 2017, http://www.latimes.com/opinion/op-ed/la-oe-olsen-democrat-immigration-strategy-20170316-story.html.

9. Paul Bedard, "Working Class Voters Flee Democrats over Support for Illegals," *Washington Examiner*, June 16, 2017, http://www.washingtonexaminer.com/working-class-voters-flee-democrats-over-partys-support-for-illegals/article/2626186.

10. Beinhart, "How the Democrats Lost Their Way."

11. Mark Krikorian, "Hail Cesar!" March 31, 2017, *National Review*, http://www.nationalreview.com/article/446311/cesar-chavez-illegal-immigration-foe.

12. Naked Emperor News, "Video Exposing How 'Occupy Wall Street' Was Organized from Day One by SEIU/ACORN Front—The Working Family Party, and How They All Tie to the Obama Administration, DNC, Democrat Socialists of America, Tides and George Soros," The Blaze, October 11, 2011, http://www.theblaze.com/news/2011/10/07/video-exposing-occupy-wall-street-was-organized-from-day-one-by-seiu-acorn-front-the-working-family-party-and-how-they-all-tie-to-the-obama-administration-dnc-democratic-socialists-of-america/.

13. Mary McHugh, "Union Head Richard Trumka Sees AFL-CIO as Socialist Vehicle," The New American, January 10, 2011, https://www.thenewamerican.com/usnews/politics/item/3651-union-head-richard-trumka-sees-afl-cio-as-socialist-vehicle.

14. David Nakamura, "AFL-CIO'S Trumka Meets with Immigrants, Calls Deportations 'Unacceptable,' *Washington Post*, April 23, 2014.

15. "Visit to Lampedusa: Homily of Holy Father Francis," Vatican, July 8, 2013, https://w2.vatican.va/content/francesco/en/homilies/2013/documents/papa-francesco_20130708_omelia-lampedusa.html.

16. John Zmirak and Jason Scott Jones, "Billionaire George Soros Tries to Mastermind the Leftward Slide of Catholics," The Stream, August 28, 2016, https://stream.org/billionaire-george-soros-masterminding-leftward-slide-catholics/.

17. Billy Hallowell, "New Book's Ironic Claim: Catholic Church Paid to Send Obama to an Alinsky-Founded Group's Community Organizing Training (See the Documents),"

The Blaze, July 23, 2012, http://www.theblaze.com/news/2012/07/23/new-books-ironic-claim-catholic-church-paid-to-send-obama-to-an-alinsky-founded-groups-community-organizing-training-see-the-documents/.

18. "Message from Modesto," World Meeting of Popular Movements, February 19, 2017, http://popularmovements.org/news/message-from-modesto/.

19. Jay Richards, "US Drops to Lowest Point Ever in Index of Economic Freedom. Can Trump Improve It?" The Stream, February 22, 2017, https://stream.org/u-s-drops-lowest-point-ever-index-economic-freedom-can-trump-improve/.

20. "Message from Modesto."

21. Charles Chaput, "Archbishop Chaput's Address at Panel Discussion on Immigration: Sanity, Indifference and the American Immigration Debate," Archdiocese of Philadelphia, September 2, 2015, http://archphila.org/2389-2/.

22. "Steve Bannon," CBS News, September 10, 2017, https://www.cbsnews.com/videos/steve-bannon/.

23. Nolan D. McCaskill, "Cardinal Dolan Rips into Bannon for 'Insulting' Remarks about Catholic Church and Immigrants," *Politico*, September 7, 2017, https://www.politico.com/story/2017/09/07/cardinal-dolan-rips-bannon-catholic-comments-242457.

24. Carlyle Murphy, "Half of U.S. Adults Raised Catholic Have Left the Church at Some Point," Pew Research, September 15, 2015, http://www.pewresearch.org/fact-tank/2015/09/15/half-of-u-s-adults-raised-catholic-have-left-the-church-at-some-point/.

25. "A Closer look at Catholic America," Pew Research, September 11, 2015, http://www.pewresearch.org/fact-tank/2015/09/14/a-closer-look-at-catholic-america/ft_15-09-11_demographicscatholicsraceimm/.

26. Anna Sutherland, "Why Latinos Are Leaving the Catholic Church," *First Things*, May 12, 2014, https://www.firstthings.com/web-exclusives/2014/05/why-latinos-are-leaving-the-catholic-church.

27. Ann Corcoran, "In 2014, Your Tax Dollars Paid 97% of the US Conference of Catholic Bishops Migration Fund Budget," Refugee Resettlement Watch, July 25, 2015, https://refugeeresettlementwatch.wordpress.com/2015/07/25/in-2014-your-tax-dollars-paid-97-of-the-us-conference-of-catholic-bishops-migration-fund-budget/.

28. Michael Sean Winters, "Bishop Paprocki's Unhinged Decree on Same-Sex Marriage," *National Catholic Reporter*, June 26, 2017, https://www.ncronline.org/blogs/distinctly-catholic/bishop-paprockis-unhinged-decree-same-sex-marriage.

29. Jack Wellman, "Top 7 Bible Verses About Immigration," Patheos, November 26, 2016, http://www.patheos.com/blogs/christiancrier/2016/11/26/top-7-bible-verses-about-immigration/.

30. Brennan Breed, "Love the Alien as Yourself: Trump, the Travel Ban and the Bible," January 20, 2017, http://www.huffingtonpost.com/brennan-breed/love-the-alien-as-yoursel_b_14480198.html.

31. James K. Hoffmeier, "The Use and Abuse of the Bible in the Immigration Debate," Center for Immigration Studies, December 1, 2011, https://cis.org/Use-and-Abuse-Bible-Immigration-Debate.

32. "A Call to Repentance & Renewal," American Association of Evangelicals, September 27, 2016, https://americanevangelicals.com/.

33. Marjorie Jeffrey, "The Evangelical Immigration Table Exposed as Another Soros Front," Juicy Ecumenism, June 5, 2013, https://juicyecumenism.com/2013/06/05/the-evangelical-immigration-table-exposed-as-another-soros-front/.

34. "Immigration in the 2106 GOP Platform," Federation for American Immigration Reform, July 19, 2016, http://immigrationreform.com/2016/07/19/immigration-in-the-2016-gop-platform/.

35. Drew DeSilver, "For Most Workers, Real Wages Have Barely Budged for Decades," Pew Research, October 9, 2014, http://www.pewresearch.org/fact-tank/2014/10/09/for-most-workers-real-wages-have-barely-budged-for-decades/.

36. "Immigration, Labor Displacement and the American Worker," Federation for American Immigration Reform, January 2016, https://fairus.org/issue/workforce-economy/immigration-labor-displacement-and-american-worker.

37. John Binder, "Open Borders Lobby, Cheap Labor Industry, Tech Giants Unite to Push Amnesty for Illegal Aliens," Breitbart, October 26, 2017, http://www.breitbart.com/big-government/2017/10/26/open-borders-lobby-cheap-labor-industrytech-giants-unite-to-push-amnesty-for-illegal-aliens/.

38. Ibid.

39. Chris Fuhrmeister, "Anthony Bourdain Hits Back at Donald Trump, Defends Immigrants," Eater, October 29, 2015, https://www.eater.com/2015/10/29/9638304/anthony-bourdain-donald-trump-immigration.

40. "2012 E-Verify Survey Summary of Results," National Restaurant Association and Immigration Works USA, April 2013, http://www.restaurant.org/Downloads/PDFs/advocacy/201304_immig_everify_survey_results.

41. Helen Raleigh, "4 Things to Know About Whether Immigrants Hurt American Workers," The Federalist, July 14, 2016, http://thefederalist.com/2016/07/14/4-things-to-know-about-whether-immigrants-hurt-american-workers/.

42. Tom Tancredo and K. C. McAlpin, "Trump Should Ignore the Business Lobby and Stick to Immigration Promises," The Hill, March 23, 2017, http://thehill.com/blogs/pundits-blog/immigration/325353-trump-should-ignore-the-business-lobby-and-stick-to.

Chapter Five: Fake Solutions to Real Problems

1. Rachel L. Swarns, "Failed Amnesty Legislation of 1986 Haunts the Current Immigration Bills in Congress," New York Times, May 23, 2006, http://www.nytimes.com/2006/05/23/washington/23amnesty.html.

2. Chuck Grassley, "Lessons Learned from the 1986 Amnesty under President Reagan," The Iowa Republican, February 4, 2013, http://theiowarepublican.com/2013/grassley-lessons-learned-from-the-1986-amnesty-under-president-reagan/.

3. Alicia A. Caldwell, "Today's Immigration Debate Rooted in 'Reagan Amnesty,' Experts Say," PBS News Hour, August 23, 2016, http://www.pbs.org/newshour/rundown/todays-immigration-debate-rooted-reagan-amnesty-experts-say/.

4. Grassley, "Lessons Learned."

5. Brad Plummer, "READ: Senators Release Bipartisan Plan for Immigration Reform," Washington Post, January 28, 2013, https://www.washingtonpost.com/news/wonk/wp/2013/01/28/read-senators-release-their-plan-for-immigration-reform/?utm_

term=.0bf63ba7d8b6; A. Kimberly Clarke, "Senators Propose Immigration Reform," *National Law Review*, January 29, 2013. https://www.natlawreview.com/node/16083.

6. David Nakamura and Ed O'Keefe, "Timeline: The Rise and Fall of Immigration Reform," *Washington Post*, June 26, 2014, https://www.washingtonpost.com/news/post-politics/wp/2014/06/26/timeline-the-rise-and-fall-of-immigration-reform/?utm_term=.e437a18e43.

7. Diana Viliers Negroponte, "The Surge in Unaccompanied Children from Central America: A Humanitarian Crisis at Our Border," June 2, 2014, https://www.brookings.edu/blog/up-front/2014/07/02/the-surge-in-unaccompanied-children-from-central-america-a-humanitarian-crisis-at-our-border.

8. Hans von Spakovsky, "DACA is Unconstitutional, as Obama Admitted," Heritage Foundation, September 8, 2017. http://www.heritage.org/immigration/commentary/daca-unconstitutional-obama-admitted.

9. Thomas Ascik, "Emotional Appeals for DACA Evade the Fact That It Is Blatantly Unconstitutional," The Federalist, September 7, 2017, http://thefederalist.com/2017/09/07/emotional-appeals-daca-evade-fact-blatantly-unconstitutional/.

10. Von Spakovsky, "DACA Is Unconstitutional."

11. "Attorney General Sessions Delivers Remarks on DACA," Department of Justice, September 5, 2017, https://www.justice.gov/opa/speech/attorney-general-sessions-delivers-remarks-daca.

12. Sophie Tatum, Daniella Diaz, and Dan Merica, "Trump, Dems Move Closer to Deal on DACA," CNN, September 14, 2017, http://www.cnn.com/2017/09/13/politics/chuck-schumer-nancy-pelosi-donald-trump/index.html.

13. Mark Abadi and Reuters, "Trump Makes Opening Demands for 'Dreamer' Deal—Including Funding for the Wall," Business Insider, October 8, 2017, http://www.cnn.com/2017/09/13/politics/chuck-schumer-nancy-pelosi-donald-trump/index.html.

14. Jerry Kammer, "Remembering Barbara Jordan and her Immigration Legacy," Center for Immigration Studies, January 17, 2016, https://cis.org/Report/Remembering-Barbara-Jordan-and-Her-Immigration-Legacy.

15. "About Us," NumbersUSA, https://www.numbersusa.com/about.

16. "Extremist Files," Southern Poverty Law Center, https://www.splcenter.org/fighting-hate/extremist-files/groups?keyword=center+for+immigration.

17. "Barbara Jordan's Vision of Immigration Reform," NumbersUSA, October 7, 2015, https://www.numbersusa.com/resource-article/barbara-jordans-vision-immigration-reform.

Chapter Six: MISSION America

1. Jerry Kramer, "Remembering Barbara Jordan and Her Immigration Legacy," Center for Immigration Studies, January 17, 2016, https://cis.org/Report/Remembering-Barbara-Jordan-and-Her-Immigration-Legacy.

2. Phil Little, Phil, *Counter Terrorism Handbook* (Nashville: Broadman and Holman Publishers, 2004), 38.

3. "Operation Gatekeeper, Operation Hold-the-Line, Operation Safeguard" GlobalSecurity, https://www.globalsecurity.org/military/ops/gatekeeper.htm.

4. Christopher Manion, "Why the Wall Will Work," Breitbart, April 14, 2016, http://www.breitbart.com/immigration/2016/04/14/why-the-wall-will-work/.

5. "Does Antonio Villaraigosa Have Two Faces?" Mayorno, http://www.mayorno.com/villar.html.

6. For the record, Zmirak favors selling California back to Mexico for one peso, and building another Wall along the San Andreas Fault.

7. Ana Campoy, "The Many and Varied Cost Estimates of Trump's Border Wall," Quartz, April 25, 2017, https://qz.com/967952/trumps-border-wall-between-the-us-and-mexico-the-many-cost-estimates-vary-widely/.

8. "Official Policy Statement: Non-Discrimination and Anti-Violence Policy," ACT for America, http://www.actforamerica.org/policy.

9. Alex Pfieffer, "New Estimate Shows It Costs Nearly $44 Billion to Educate Illegal Aliens Annually," The Daily Caller, September 14, 2016, http://dailycaller.com/2016/09/14/new-estimate-shows-it-costs-nearly-44-billion-to-educate-illegal-aliens-annually/.

10. Catalina Gonella, "Visa Overstays Outnumber Illegal Border Crossings, Trend Expected to Continue," NBC News, March 7, 2017, https://www.nbcnews.com/news/latino/visa-overstays-outnumber-illegal-border-crossings-trend-expected-continue-n730216.

11. Joshua Gilln, "Rubio says 40% of Illegal Immigrants Stayed in the U.S. after Their Visas Expired," Politifact Florida, July 29, 2015, http://www.politifact.com/florida/statements/2015/jul/29/marco-rubio/rubio-says-40-percent-illegal-immigrants-are-overs.

12. David Nield, "Use These Six Apps to Track Friends and Family on a Map," gizmodo.com, January 5, 2016, http://fieldguide.gizmodo.com/6-apps-to-track-friends-and-family-on-a-map-1751084283.

13. Stephen Dinan, "Staggering Number of Visa Overstays Now Biggest Problem in Illegal Immigration, *Washington Times*, May 22, 2017, http://www.washingtontimes.com/news/2017/may/22/visa-overstays-biggest-problem-illegal-immigration/.

14. Ibid.

15. "Identity and Immigration Status of 9/11 Terrorists," Federation for American Immigration Reform, January 2011, https://fairus.org/issue/national-security/identity-and-immigration-status-911-terrorists.

16. "S.F. 'Sanctuary' Policy Violates Common Sense," *USA Today*, July 15, 2015, https://www.usatoday.com/story/opinion/2015/07/15/immigration-sanctuary-shooting-steinle-lopez-sanchez-editorials-debates/30100967/.

17. Elizabeth Zwirtz, "Steinle's Accused Killer Found Not Guilty of Murder, to Be Deported," Fox News, November 30, 2017, http://www.foxnews.com/us/2017/11/30/kate-steinle-s-accused-killer-found-not-guilty-murder.html.

18. Hans A. von Spakovsky and Grant Strobl, "What the Media Won't Tell You About Legal Immigration and Criminal Activity," Heritage Foundation, March 13, 2017, http://www.heritage.org/immigration/commentary/what-the-media-wont-tell-you-about-illegal-immigration-and-criminal-activity.

19. Stephen Dinan, "Trump Presses More Countries [to] Take Back U.S. Deportees in Immigration Success," May 16, 2017, http://www.washingtontimes.com/news/2017/may/16/countries-refusing-us-deportees-cut-from-20-to-12/.

20. Joe Guzzardi, "Identity Theft an Overlooked Wrinkle of Illegal Immigration," *USA Today*, July 3, 2017, https://www.usatoday.com/story/opinion/columnists/2017/07/03/identity-theft-overlooked-wrinkle-illegal-immigration/444863001/.

21. Ronald W. Mortensen, "Illegal, but Not Undocumented," Center for Immigration Studies, June 19, 2009, https://cis.org/Report/Illegal-Not-Undocumented.

22. Ibid.

23. Ibid.

24. Steve Lopez, "Not Legal but Need a License?" *Los Angeles Times*, September 5, 2004, http://articles.latimes.com/2004/sep/05/local/me-lopez5.

25. "Federal Identity Theft Laws," Office for Victims of Crime, October 2010, https://www.ovc.gov/pubs/ID_theft/idtheftlaws.html.

26. Chalres Doyle, "Mandatory Minimum Sentencing for Federal Aggravated Identity Theft," Congressional Research Service, August 20, 2015, https://fas.org/sgp/crs/misc/R42100.pdf.

27. "E-Verify," Department of Homeland Security, https://www.uscis.gov/e-verify.

28. Ibid.

29. "Assembly Bill No. 1236," Official California Legislative Information, May 19, 2011, http://leginfo.ca.gov/pub/11-12/bill/asm/ab_1201-1250/ab_1236_bill_20110909_enrolled.pdf.

30. Alexandra Marks, "With E-Verify, Too Many Errors to Expand Its Use?" *Christian Science Monitor*, July 8, 2008, https://www.csmonitor.com/USA/2008/0707/p02s01-usgn.html.

31. "How Do You Report Suspected Tax Fraud Activity?" IRS, https://www.irs.gov/individuals/how-do-you-report-suspected-tax-fraud-activity.

32. Aaron Zitnor, "Birthright Citizenship by the Numbers," *Wall Street Journal*, August 20, 2015, https://blogs.wsj.com/briefly/2015/08/20/birthright-citizenship-by-the-numbers-the-numbers.

33. Ibid.

34. Jon Feere, "Birthright Citizenship in the United States: A Global Comparison," Center for Immigration Studies, August 31, 2010, https://cis.org/Birthright-Citizenship-United-States.

35. Ibid.

36. Ibid.

37. Jessica Vaughn, "Immigration Multipliers: Trends in Chain Migration," Center for Immigration Studies, September 27, 2017, https://cis.org/Report/Immigration-Multipliers.

38. Steve Cortes, "End Chain Migration, As Trump Wants, and Switch to Merit-Based Immigration," Fox News, December 20, 2017, http://www.foxnews.com/opinion/2017/12/20/end-chain-migration-as-trump-wants-and-switch-to-merit-based-immigration.html.

39. Ramah McKay, "Family Reunification," Migration Policy Institute, May 1, 2003, https://www.migrationpolicy.org/article/family-reunification.

40. Stephen Dinan and Sally Persons, "Trump Points to Terror Attempt as Reason to End Visa Lottery, Chain Migration," *Washington Times*, December 11, 2017, https://www.washingtontimes.com/news/2017/dec/11/trump-chain-migration-blame-nyc-terrorist-attack/.

41. Julie Manchester, "DHS Labels Pennsylvania Shootings a Terror Attack, Blasts Chain Migration," *The Hill*, December 24, 2017, http://thehill.com/blogs/blog-briefing-room/news/366350-dhs-labels-pennsylvania-shooting-a-terror-attack.

42. "S.354 RAISE Act," Congress, https://www.congress.gov/bill/115th-congress/senate-bill/354.

43. Hrishikesh Joshi, "Does the 'Diversity' Lottery Live Up to Its Name?" *The Hill*, January 15, 2016, http://thehill.com/blogs/congress-blog/foreign-policy/265964-does-the-diversity-lottery-live-up-to-its-name.

44. Travis Fedschun, "NYC Terror Attack suspect, Sayfullo Saipov, Entered US through Diversity Visa Program," Fox News, November 1, 2017, http://www.foxnews.com/us/2017/11/01/nyc-terror-attack-suspect-sayfullo-saipov-entered-us-through-diversity-visa-program.html.

45. Robert VerBruggen, "The Cotton/Perdue Immigration Plan Is a Great Start," *National Review*, August 2, 2017, http://www.nationalreview.com/article/450061/cotton-perdues-immigration-plan-emphasize-skills

46. Jimmy Carter, "Sanctions Against Iran Remarks Announcing U.S. Actions," The American Presidency Project, April 7, 1980. http://www.presidency.ucsb.edu/ws/?pid=33233%2.

47. Patrick Howley, "Flashback: FDR Suspends Japanese, German Immigration by Executive Order," Breitbart, December 9, 2015, http://www.breitbart.com/big-government/2015/12/09/flashback-fdr-suspends-japanese-german-immigration-executive-order/.

48. Jessica Vaughn, "Study Reveals 72 Terrorists Came from Countries Covered by Trump Vetting Order," Center for Immigration Studies, February 11, 2017, https://cis.org/Vaughan/Study-Reveals-72-Terrorists-Came-Countries-Covered-Trump-Vetting-Order.

49. Rowan Scarborough, "Islamic State Finds Success Infiltrating Its Terrorists into Refugee Flows to the West," *Washington Times*, January 29, 2017, http://www.washingtontimes.com/news/2017/jan/29/isis-finds-success-infiltrating-terrorists-into-re/.

50. Jim Brunsden, "Europe Refugee Policy Is 'Trojan Horse of Terrorism', Says Orban," *Financial Times*, March 30, 2017, https://www.ft.com/content/538b2a0a-154e-11e7-80f4-13e067d5072c.

51. Baron Bodissey, "Criticizing Immigration Is a Criminal Offense in Bavaria," Gates of Vienna, July 12, 2016, http://gatesofvienna.net/2016/07/criticizing-immigration-is-a-criminal-offense-in-bavaria/.

52. Tom Parfitt, "German Cop faces CRIMINAL CHARGES for calling Angela Merkel 'INSANE'" *Express* (U.K.), December 23, 2016, http://www.express.co.uk/news/world/746883/Angela-Merkel-Germany-police-refugee-migrant-crisis-AFD-Berlin-terror-attack.

53. Ayaan Hirsi Ali, "How to Counter Political Islam," Hoover Institution, March 22, 2017, https://www.hoover.org/research/how-counter-political-islam.

54. "Background Note on the Safe Country Concept and Refugee Status, EC/SCP/68," UNHCR, July 26, 1991, http://www.unhcr.org/en-us/excom/scip/3ae68ccec/background-note-safe-country-concept-refugee-status.html.

55. Denis MacEoin, "The Arab States and the Refugees," Gatestone Institute, September 16, 2016, https://www.gatestoneinstitute.org/6502/refugees-arab-states.

56. Steven A. Camorata, "The High Cost of Resettling Middle East Refugees," Center for Immigration Studies, November 4, 2015, https://cis.org/Report/High-Cost-Resettling-Middle-Eastern-Refugees.

57. Rachel Stoltzfoos, "Let's Be Real: Obama 'Barred' Syrian Christian Refugees," The Daily Caller News Foundation, January 29, 2017, https://stream.org/lets-real-obama-barred-syrian-christian-refugees/.

58. Chris Enloe, "See Just How Much Trump Has Slashed Refugee Resettlement in U.S.—the Numbers Are Astounding," The Blaze, December 6, 2017, http://www.theblaze.com/news/2017/12/06/see-just-how-much-trump-has-slashed-refugee-resettlement-in-u-s-the-numbers-are-astounding/?utm_source=dlvr.it&utm_medium=twitter.

59. "Public Charge," U.S Citizenship and Immigration Services, https://www.uscis.gov/greencard/public-charge.

60. Ibid.

Chapter Seven: How to Sell Reality to People Allergic to Facts

1. Eleanor Goldberg, "80 Percent of Central American Women, Girls are Raped Crossing into the U.S.", Huffington Post, September 12, 2014, https://www.huffingtonpost.com/2014/09/12/central-america-migrants-rape_n_5806972.html.

2. Based on an average premium cost of $833 for an unsubsidized family from Matt O'Brien and Spencer Raley, "How Much Does Health Insurance Cost without a Subsidy?" eHealth Insurance Resource Center, October 10, 2016, https://resources.ehealthinsurance.com/affordable-care-act/much-health-insurance-cost-without-subsidy.

3. Julia Edwards Ainsley, "Exclusive—Trump Border 'Wall' to Cost $21.6 Billion, Take 3.5 Years to Build: Internal Report," Reuters, February 9, 2017, http://www.reuters.com/article/us-usa-trump-immigration-wall-exclusive/exclusive-trump-border-wall-to-cost-21-6-billion-take-3-5-years-to-build-internal-report-idUSKBN15O2ZN. Based on the average teacher salary of $56,383 from "Teacher Salaries in America," Niche, https://articles.niche.com/teacher-salaries-in-america/, and an estimate provided by School Planning and Management putting the median cost of building a middle school at $26.5 million.

4. Matt O'Brien and Spencer Raley, "The Fiscal Burden of Illegal Immigration on United States Taxpayers," Federation for American Immigration Reform, September 27, 2017, https://fairus.org/issue/publications-resources/fiscal-burden-illegal-immigration-united-states-taxpayers.

5. Dres Desilver, "For Most Workers, Real Wages Have Barely Budged for Decades," Pew Research Center, October 9, 2014, http://www.pewresearch.org/fact-tank/2014/10/09/for-most-workers-real-wages-have-barely-budged-for-decades/.

6. Elise Gould, "Poor People Work," Economic Policy Institute, May 19, 2015, http://www.epi.org/publication/poor-people-work-a-majority-of-poor-people-who-can-work-do/.

7. Hans A. von Spakovsky, "What the Media Won't Tell You about Illegal Immigration and Criminal Activity," Heritage Foundation, March 13, 2017, http://www.heritage.org/immigration/commentary/what-the-media-wont-tell-you-about-illegal-immigration-and-criminal-activity.

8. "Criminal Alien Statistics: Information on Incarceration, Arrests, and Costs," United States Government Accountability Office, March 2011, http://www.gao.gov/ assets/320/316959.pdf.

9. Tinao Sanandaji, "What Is the Truth about Crime and Immigration in Sweden?" *National Review*, February 25, 2017, http://www.nationalreview.com/article/445237/ sweden-crime-rates-statistics-immigration-trump-fox-news. That 2005 study showed foreigners were four times more likely to be suspects in homicide cases, and 4.5 times more in rape cases.

10. David Barrett, "Violent Crime Jumps 27 per cent in New Figures Released by the Office for National Statistics," Telegraph, January 22, 2016, http://www.telegraph. co.uk/news/uknews/crime/12112024/Violent-crime-jumps-27-in-new-figures.html.

11. Jan Cienski, "Why Poland Doesn't Want Refugees," *Politico*, May 21, 2017, https:// www.politico.eu/article/politics-nationalism-and-religion-explain-why-poland-doesnt-want-refugees/.

12. "Poland 2016 Crime & Safety Report," United States Department of State Bureau of Diplomatic Security, https://www.osac.gov/pages/ContentReportDetails.aspx?cid =19148.

13. "The Muslim Brotherhood's Strategic Plan for America—Court Document," Clarion Project, https://clarionproject.org/muslim_brotherhood_explanatory_memorandum/.

14. "Mexican Aliens Seek to Retake 'Stolen' Land," *Washington Times*, April 16, 2006, https://www.washingtontimes.com/news/2006/apr/16/20060416-122222-1672r/.

15. Carlyle Murphy, "Half of U.S. Adults Raised Catholic Have Left the Church at Some Point," Pew Research, September 15, 2015, http://www.pewresearch.org/fact-tank/2015/09/15/half-of-u-s-adults-raised-catholic-have-left-the-church-at-some-point/; "A Closer Look at Catholic America," Pew Research, September 11, 2015, http://www.pewresearch.org/fact-tank/2015/09/14/a-closer-look-at-catholic-america/ ft_15-09-11_demographicscatholicsraceimm/.

16. Mary Anne Hackett, "Follow the Money Trail," CatholicCitizens.org, April 14, 2017, https://catholiccitizens.org/views/70700/follow-money-trail/; Migration and Refugee Services Annual Report, USCCB, 2014, http://www.usccb.org/about/migration-and-refugee-services/annual-report.cfm.

17. "Christian Leaders Warn of Soros-Funded "Hijack" of Christian Left," The Stream, October 4, 2016, https://stream.org/christian-leaders-warn-of-progressive-attempt-to-hijack-the-gospel/.

18. "Second generation immigrants typically have higher crime rates than first-generation immigrants." In Europe, "some second-generation immigrant groups have crime rates that drastically exceed those of the native born population." These second-generation immigrants involved in crime are disproportionately Muslim. Krishnadev Calamur, "Are Immigrants Prone to Crime and Terrorism?" *Atlantic*, June 15, 2016, https:// www.theatlantic.com/news/archive/2016/06/immigrants-and-crime/486884/, quoting Sandra M. Bucerius, *Oxford Handbook of Crime and Criminal Justice*.

19. Sofia Lotto Persio, "Crime in Mexico: Murder Rate Reaches Record High and Nobody Is Talking about It," *Newsweek*, June 22, 2017, http://www.newsweek.com/crime-mexico-murder-rate-reaches-record-high-and-nobody-talking-about-it-628193.

20. "Andrew Becker and Patrick J. McDonnell, "Mexico's Drug War Creates New Class of Refugees," *Los Angeles Times*, March 4, 2009, http://www.latimes.com/world/mexico-americas/la-na-asylum4-2009mar04-story.html.

21. Ronald Reagan, "A Nation That Cannot Control Its Borders Is Not a Nation," AZ Quotes, http://www.azquotes.com/quote/371938.

22. Ed Stetzer, "My Stance on Refugees and Immigration, and How They Intersect with Christianity," *Christianity Today*, May 5, 2017, http://www.christianitytoday.com/edstetzer/2017/may/my-stance-on-refugees-and-immigration-and-how-they-intersec.html

23. Saagar Enjeti, "London Police Chief: Terror Victims Show How Diverse We Are," The Daily Caller News Foundation, June 11, 2017, http://dailycaller.com/2017/06/11/london-police-chief-terror-victims-show-how-diverse-we-are/.

24. Terence P. Jeffrey, "Gallup: Nearly 710 Million Would-Be Migrants—147M Want to Go to USA; 39M Germany; 36M Canada; 35M UK; 32M France," CNS News, June 9, 2017, https://www.cnsnews.com/news/article/terence-p-jeffrey/710-million-would-be-migrants-147m-want-go-usa-39m-germany-36m-canada.

Index